border to border · teen to teen · border to border · teen to teen · border to border

TEENS IN THE PHILIPPINES

Teens in the Philippines

Philippines

by Jason Skog

Content Adviser: James F. Eder,
Professor of Anthropology,
Arizona State University

Reading Adviser: Alexa L. Sandmann, Ed.D.,
Professor of Literacy, College and
Graduate School of Education,
Kent State University

Compass Point Books ✦ Minneapolis, Minnesota

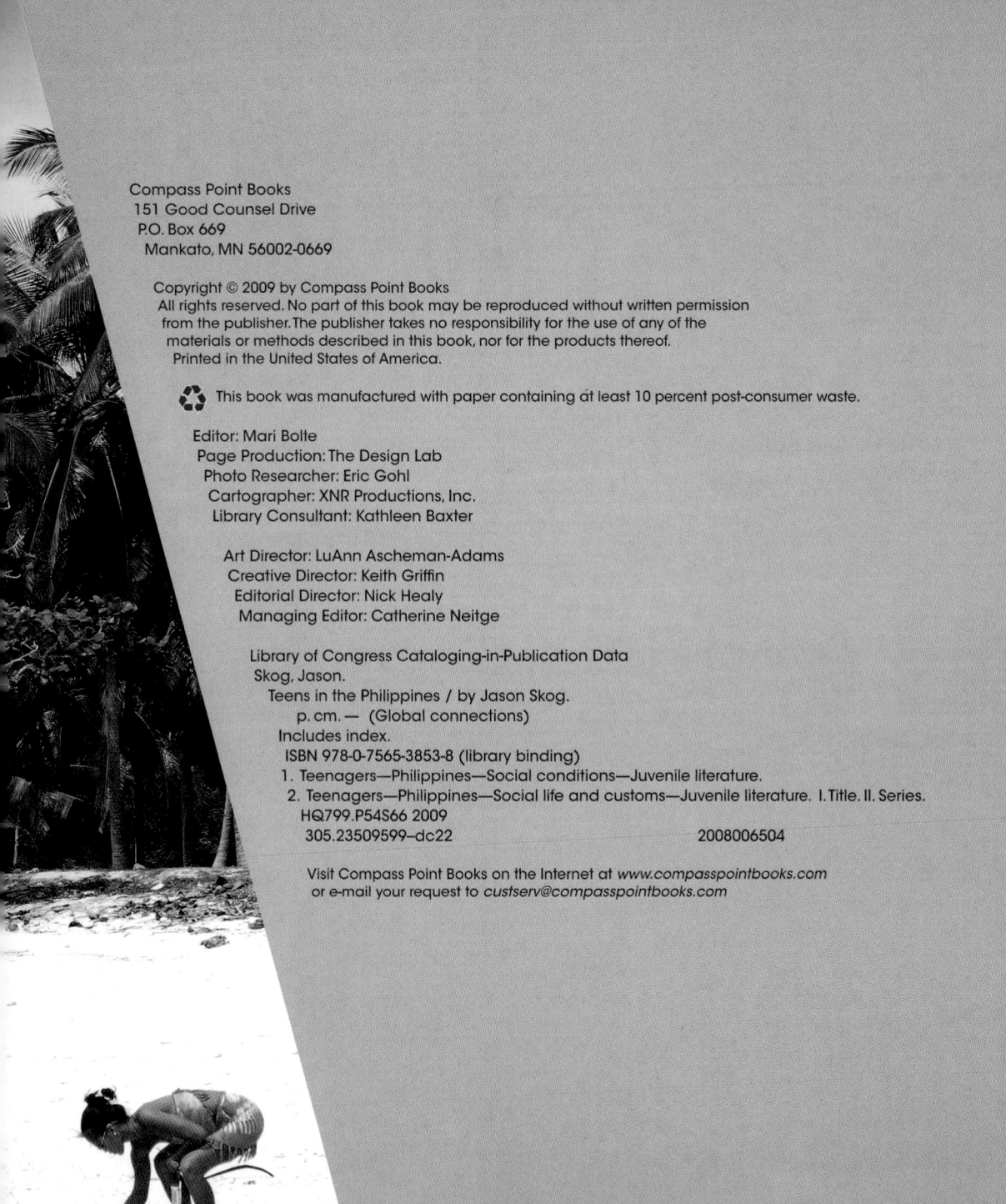

Compass Point Books
151 Good Counsel Drive
P.O. Box 669
Mankato, MN 56002-0669

This book was manufactured with paper containing at least 10 percent post-consumer waste.

Editor: Mari Bolte
Page Production: The Design Lab
Photo Researcher: Eric Gohl
Cartographer: XNR Productions, Inc.
Library Consultant: Kathleen Baxter

Art Director: LuAnn Ascheman-Adams
Creative Director: Keith Griffin
Editorial Director: Nick Healy
Managing Editor: Catherine Neitge

Library of Congress Cataloging-in-Publication Data
Skog, Jason.
    Teens in the Philippines / by Jason Skog.
        p. cm. — (Global connections)
    Includes index.
    ISBN 978-0-7565-3853-8 (library binding)
    1. Teenagers—Philippines—Social conditions—Juvenile literature.
    2. Teenagers—Philippines—Social life and customs—Juvenile literature. I. Title. II. Series.
    HQ799.P54S66 2009
    305.23509599—dc22   2008006504

Visit Compass Point Books on the Internet at www.compasspointbooks.com
or e-mail your request to custserv@compasspointbooks.com

Table of Contents

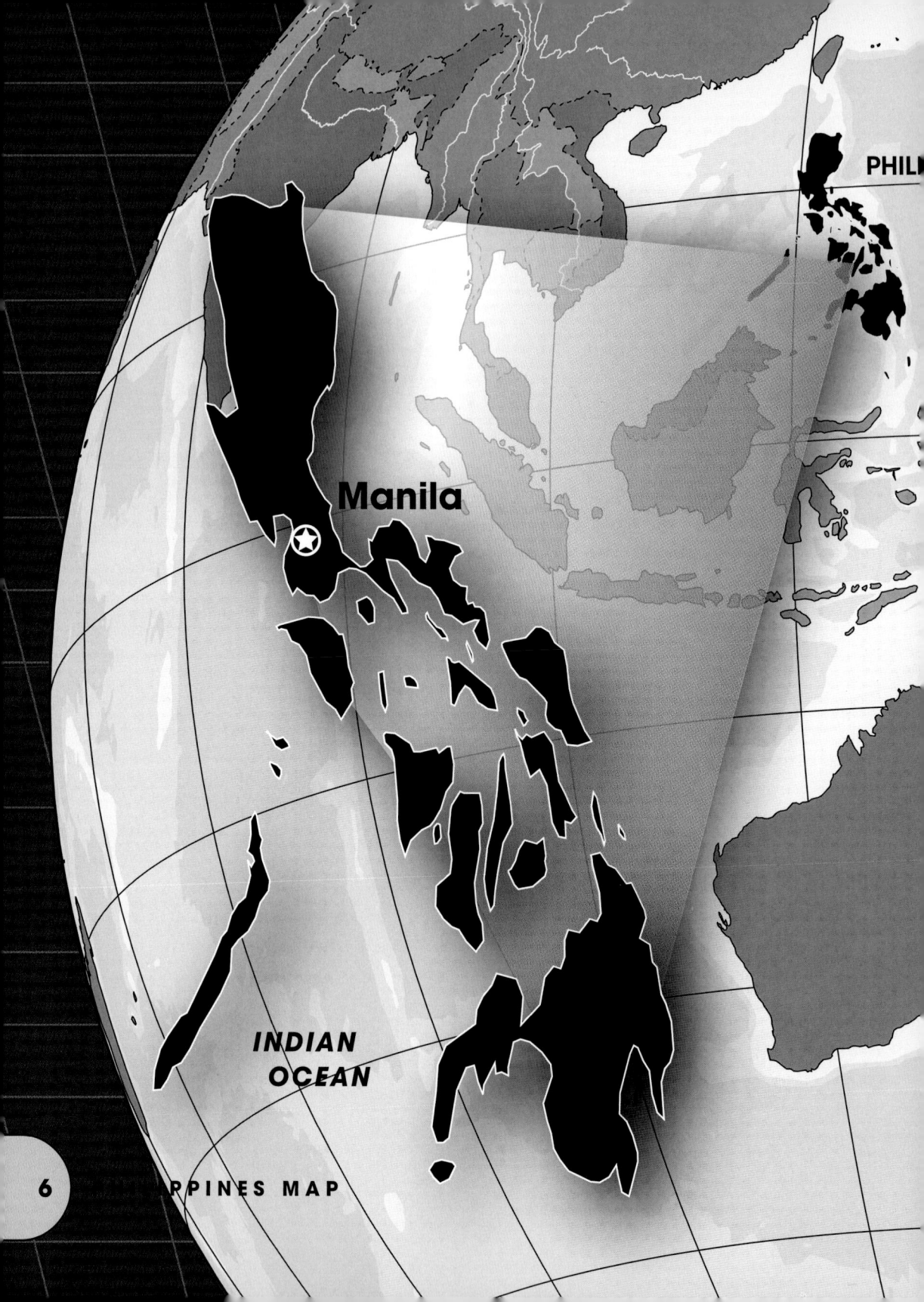

PHILI

Manila

*INDIAN
OCEAN*

PPINES MAP

PACIFIC
OCEAN

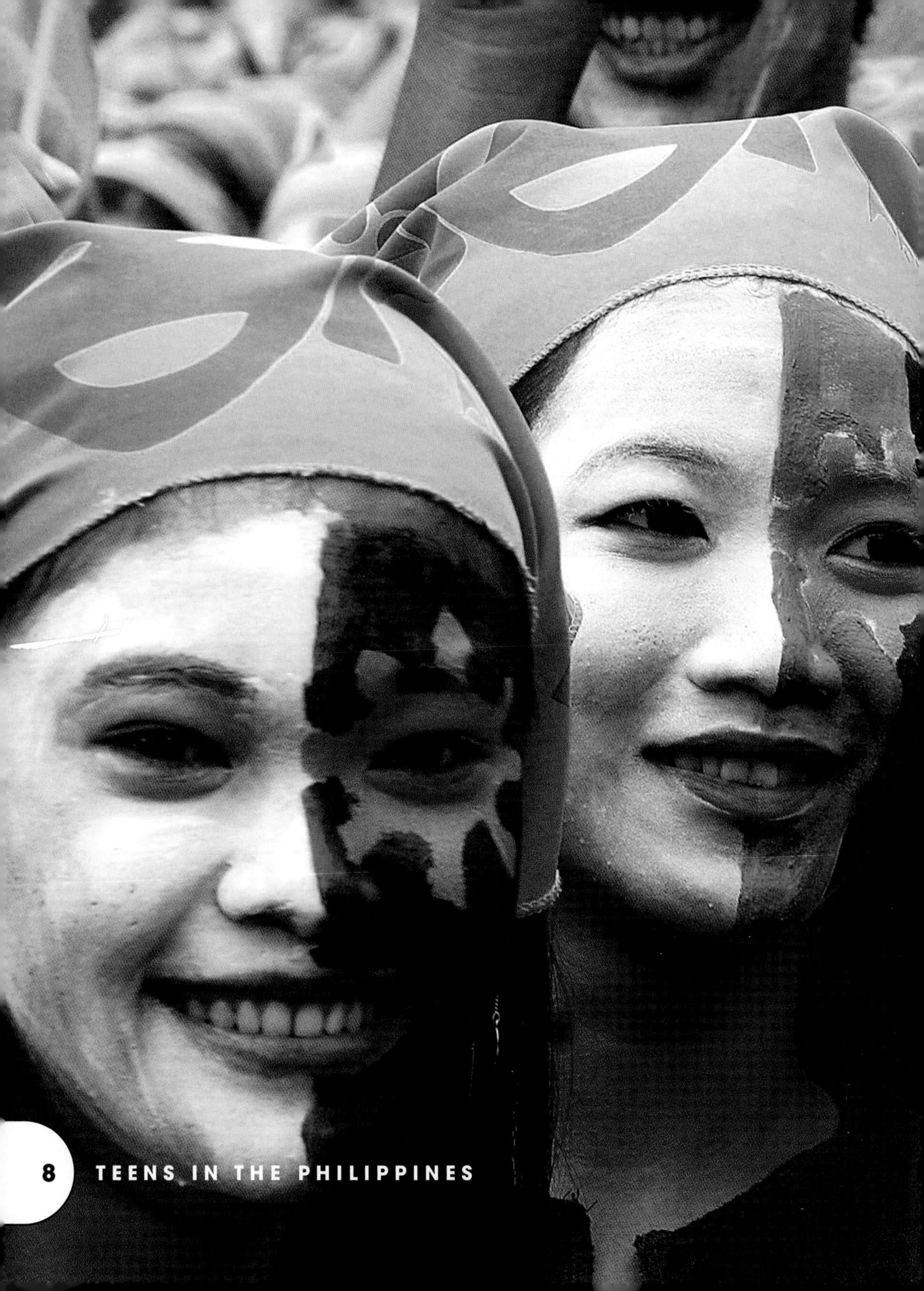

SO MANY SMILES SPREAD ACROSS THE MANY FACES IN THE PHILIPPINES THAT THIS SOUTHEAST ASIAN NATION IS CONSIDERED ONE OF THE HAPPIEST COUNTRIES IN THE WORLD. The Philippines is the 12th most densely populated country in the world, with more than 91 million residents. Nearly 9 million of these are between the ages of 15 and 19, and all lead diverse and dynamic lives.

The 7,107 islands of the Philippines were formed by volcanic activity millions of years ago. Roughly 4,000 of the nation's islands have names, and people inhabit about 1,000 of them. The experiences of teens in the Philippines vary greatly, depending on where they live. City teens have education, entertainment, culture, and commerce at their disposal. Rural teens may have limited access to schools, electricity, and technology.

The differences in lifestyles between the lower and upper economic classes are striking. Poverty plagues almost 40 percent of Filipino families. Yet most teens lead active, happy lives surrounded by large, loving families.

Although in the past educational standards have been different for boys and girls, the government has been trying to make the classes more even—especially in recent years, when girls are more likely to stay in school.

CHAPTER ONE

Learning in Spite of Obstacles

STUDENTS FILE INTO THEIR CLASSROOM AND TAKE A SEAT AT WOODEN DESKS AND CHAIRS. Their teacher enters the room and calls the students to order. In the Philippines, students address their female teachers as "mum," a variation of "ma'am." Male teachers are called "sir." Both are titles that teachers are happy to hear, and they even use them to address each other.

The school day begins at 7:30 A.M. with a brief ceremony that includes raising the flag, singing the national anthem, reciting the pledge of allegiance, and saying a prayer. Both public and private schools have paintings of the Virgin Mary in the classrooms and quiet areas for prayer.

The school week runs from Monday through Friday, with each class day ending between 4:30 and 5 P.M. Students usually have 60 to 90 minutes for lunch, but most schools do not serve meals. Children usually bring a sack lunch from home, wait for their mothers to bring them

The Philippines and the United States are the only two countries to have a pledge of allegiance.

a hot meal, or walk home to eat with their families. Some students may grab a quick bite to eat from a snack stand outside the school run by the parent-teacher association or a street vendor.

Rural Education

Education is considered the best way for Filipinos to get ahead in life. Students must attend school until they are 12 years old. Around half of those

Teen Scenes

It's a little before 7 A.M. A 14-year-old boy hurries out of his family's high-rise apartment building in downtown Manila. He's running late for school. The city streets are already clogged with buses, cars, and taxis. He hops on a bus for a 30-minute ride through heavy traffic and gets to school just in time. At lunchtime, he and his friends grab a snack from a vendor's cart. While they eat, they make plans to play basketball later in the week.

When he gets home, his mother has chores that need to be done. He tackles a stack of homework and then plays his favorite video game before watching a little TV. He finally turns out the lights around 10 P.M.

On the island of Palawan in the west central portion of the Philippines, a 13-year-old girl wakes up in her family's modest bamboo, wood, and straw *nipa* hut. She must fetch a pail of clean water so her mother can cook breakfast. After a quick meal of rice, the girl washes up and starts her 40-minute walk to school.

nipa
NEE-pah

A group of the girl's friends is waiting for her. Together, they head into the school, a crowded, dirt-floor building without electricity. When her classes are over, she stops at a friend's hut on her way home to skip rope and play a quick game of *piko*, a game similar to hopscotch. But she soon heads home. Her parents need help tending to the family's rice paddies, where tiny kernels of rice grow in the shallow water. After helping her mother set out dinner, she finishes her homework and reads the latest edition of her favorite comic book. Then she turns out the light and drifts off to sleep.

piko
PEE-koh

In the far north, deep in the rainforest of the Sierra Madre mountain range on the island of Luzon, a storm wakes a 15-year-old boy from his deep sleep. Built on sturdy ironwood posts, the house is under constant attack from rain. The moisture causes the house to slowly rot. He no longer attends school, but instead walks through the dense forests each day gathering rattan with his father. His family uses the sturdy, vinelike plant to make furniture and baskets. They sell their products at the market so they can buy food and clothing.

From city to country and island to island, these teens have diverse lifestyles. Regardless of their situation in life, their Filipino heritage ties them together.

Help From an Early Age

Infant mortality is always a concern in the Philippines, so adults stay close by their newborns. Babies are carefully watched and protected, often while they are asleep.

From the moment they are born, Filipino children are both protected from and exposed to the world around them. The mother, father, or another adult carries the child, who is included in almost every activity in daily life. There is no pressure for a child to "grow up" and learn new skills, yet babies and young children learn by watching adults interact.

The ultimate goal of such care and attention is to give the child a head start by the time he or she enters school. This also gives children a sense of security and self-esteem. More than 90 percent of Filipinos can read and write by the time they are 10 years old.

The Philippines' high birth rate adds many students to the education system each year. The increasing numbers strain resources and crowd classrooms. As a result, classes in some areas are taught in shifts. One group of students attends morning classes, while another arrives for instruction in the afternoon.

students continue on to secondary school. One-tenth of all students will finish college.

However, in rural areas, students are less likely to stay in school past the age of 12. This is because teens are needed to help on family farms. In the poorest areas, nearly 40 percent of children do not attend school at all. Of the roughly 13 million Filipino students who attend elementary school, nearly 9 percent drop out before they finish the required six years of education. By the time students are old enough for secondary education (ages 13 to 16), enrollment drops to around 6.3 million.

Public schools usually do not offer preschool or kindergarten classes. However, children with wealthy parents might attend private preschool and kindergarten when they are 4 and 5 years old.

For most students, school begins with first grade when they turn 6 and continues through sixth grade. Secondary education, which is not required, begins at age 13 and lasts four years.

Covering the Basics

April and May are the hottest months in the Philippines. The school year runs from June to March to avoid the heat. However, June is the start of the wet, "rainy" season, and some older schools in low-lying areas are vulnerable to flooding.

The academic calendar is 200 days long, with a two- to three-week break

Leading Languages

The Philippines has 11 written and spoken languages and 80 or more dialects. (There is a variety of estimates regarding the number of dialects in the Philippines, depending on how "dialect" and "language" are defined. Some estimate there are as few as 60 dialects, while others guess at more than 170.) Still, Filipino and English are the two official languages. Children learn them at home and in school. Both languages are taught, starting in the first grade. TV, radio, and newspapers are in both English and Filipino.

The Filipino language is based on Tagalog, the native language of the Philippines. The word comes from *tagá-ílog*, a combination of tagá, or "native of," and ílog, meaning "river" or "river dweller." Many Tagalog words are borrowed from other languages, including Spanish, Arabic, Chinese, and Sanskrit.

English is spoken by more than half of Filipinos. The Philippines is the third-largest English-speaking country in the world, after the United States and Canada. English is used in the classroom to teach reading, science, and math. It has become more common at colleges and universities because the Filipino language lacks words for some scientific and technological terms. In some areas, Filipinos are embracing "Taglish," a combination of Filipino and English.

tagá-ílog
tah-GAH-Elug

The Earliest Educators

Centuries before the arrival of Spanish conquerors in 1521, the people of Ilocos on the northern island of Luzon were using an informal education system. They used it to teach children their history, folktales, and mythological stories.

Stories of the mythical character Lam-ang and his control over the natives of the island of Luzon were passed down from generation to generation. Children learned other aspects of their people's history through poetry, songs, and dances about religion, folk heroes, art, love, war, and the seasonal harvest. Parents and tribal elders were responsible for relating these tales to young people. This is a tradition that still continues in some remote areas.

In 1611, the college of Santo Tomas was founded in Manila. It became a university in 1645, making it one of the oldest higher-education institutions in the world. In 1863, a law was passed that ordered every parish, or regional territory of the Catholic Church, to have its own school.

In 2006, the Philippines was hit by three large typhoons in a span of 10 weeks. The typhoons caused more than 2.5 billion pesos (U.S.$60 million) in damage to school buildings alone.

in December. Another weeklong break comes in November to mark the Day of the Saints and the Day of the Dead. The size of the average classroom varies dramatically, depending on whether the school is in the city or the country, private or public. In poorer rural areas, classrooms are typically smaller and may lack electricity. Many have dirt floors and become flooded during the rainy season. Computers, once rare in all but the most prestigious private schools, are becoming more common in schools, and the government is looking for ways to pay for new technology.

The Philippines has some of the most crowded classrooms in Asia. Public classrooms can have 50 students or more. Crowded urban areas often have more students, while rural areas have fewer students. In larger classes, books and desks are sometimes shared.

School subjects include English, mathematics, and Makabayan, which is a combination of social studies and Filipino language courses. Science, music, arts, and physical education are also part of the curriculum. Private elementary school students typically have smaller class sizes and may study arts, computers, health, and other languages in addition to the basic courses provided in public schools.

In 2006, more than 45,000 Filipinos were evacuated when it appeared as though the Mayon Volcano on the island of Luzon might erupt. The Mayon Volcano is the most active volcano in the Philippines. Temporary schools were set up at evacuation centers so school could continue uninterrupted.

The Next Step

When a student begins secondary education, the course offerings become broader and more challenging. In addition to the main courses, students might also study health, advanced computers, music, arts, technology, home economics, and physical education. Basic subjects become increasingly difficult; math students start with algebra but eventually move up to calculus, while science students begin with basic science but end their education with physics.

What They're Wearing

Many Filipino students have to wear uniforms to class, and students who cannot afford the proper clothing are not allowed to attend. However, many public elementary schools don't require uniforms because not all families can

Secondary Education Courses

Year 1	Year 2	Year 3	Year 4
algebra	geometry	trigonometry	calculus
science	biology	chemistry	physics
English I	English II	American literature	world literature
Filipino I	Filipino II	Filipino III	Filipino IV
Philippines history	Asian history	world history	economics

Some teens like school uniforms because they take the guesswork out of what to wear. Others are less positive. One teen said, "It's quite a challenge to make yourself stand out in a school where everyone wears the same clothes."

afford the expense. But nearly all high schools require uniforms. The poorest students often have only one outfit. This is because a single uniform costs around 135 pesos (U.S.$3.25), which is nearly a day's wages for some workers. Girls wear pleated skirts and white blouses. If they attend public school, their skirts are all the same color. Boys wear white shirts and dark pants. Private schools have their own colors for shirts, skirts, and pants.

Teachers also are required to wear uniforms, and the government gives them an allowance to buy up to four each year. Women dress like their female pupils. Men dress in dark pants and either a polo shirt or a *barong*, a light cotton shirt.

When they are not in school, teens favor clothing worn in Western countries. Jeans are favorite choices for boys, with a T-shirt or sports jersey on top. Girls also wear jeans, but they are more likely to opt for a skirt or slacks with a blouse. In rural areas or mountainous regions, Filipino

barong
bah-RONG

The barong tagalog became the official national costume of the Philippines in 1975.

teens sometimes combine traditional dress with Western clothing.

For young women, a *terno* is a popular option. The form-fitting dress is ankle-length and adorned with colorful embroidery or hand-painted flowers. Some fancier ternos, worn to more formal affairs and festivals, have pearls, beads, and sequins. Ternos have long, flowing sleeves that set them apart from most formal dresses in the West.

For young men, the *barong tagalog* is the shirt of choice for formal functions. This loose-knit shirt has ornate embroidery. In urban areas, it has been adapted for everyday use as a short, snugger shirt.

terno
TERE-noh
barong tagalog
bah-RONG tah-GAH-lug

Graduation and Higher Education

Once they finish secondary school, students have the option to continue their education. Some apply for admission to a college or university in the city. Although the cost is high, a college graduate has higher earning potential than a person without a college degree. Students and their families see higher education as a good investment.

The number of Filipino students getting degrees in information technology has exploded recently. Many high-tech graduates move to neighboring Asian countries or overseas to work in the growing field. Other students opt for technical school to learn trades like mechanical or electrical work, hair-dressing, plumbing, and appliance or computer repair.

Staying Busy After School

When the bell signals the end of another school day, many Filipino teens head for their favorite club, go to a job, or play an after-school sport. Few Filipino schools have the money to offer many organized after-school activities, so students turn to clubs, community groups, and their friends for entertainment. Some larger cities host chess, acting, and dance clubs. Other teens get together for a quick game of no-rules basketball or head to the nearest river or pond for a refreshing swim.

There are more than 2,000 higher education institutions throughout the Philippines.

Despite the mountainous terrain, around 14 percent of the 98,460 miles (158,810 kilometers) of road in the Philippines is paved, making it easier to get around.

2

A Life of Smiles

DEPENDING ON WHETHER TEENS LIVE IN A CROWDED CITY OR ON A QUIET FARM, THEIR LIVES VARY GREATLY.

Yet they all seem to share some traits. Most come from large, supportive families, value education, and manage not to take themselves too seriously. When it comes to having fun, one teen writes that the options are many:

Here in the Philippines there sure are so many exciting things to do ... sometimes we stick around at home and have fun with family or hang out with same-age neighbors (if there happen to be any), but that is not everything to it ... if we feel like sitting down ... we resort to watching our favorite shows on TV, ... switch on the computer, ... log on to Friendster, IM our friends, or ... spend the whole day typing around on our cell phones.

Rise and Shine

For most Filipino teens, the day starts early. Breakfast is served around 6 A.M. Meals usually are made from leftovers from the night before and are typically not reheated. On special occasions, breakfast might include eggs and sausage. Teens in a hurry often grab a quick breakfast from a vending cart on their way to school, usually a small bun called a *pan de sal*.

At midmorning and in the afternoon, they head outside or to a nearby café for a snack break called a *merienda*. Foods for the merienda are usually sweet and include a drink made from instant coffee, evaporated milk, and sugar. Students

pan de sal
pan-de-SAHL
merienda
merry-enda

also are served doughnuts and other sweet rolls, or a noodle dish.

Midday and Evening Meals

At home, lunch is usually a light meal of rice and a side dish of fish, vegetables, or meat. Coca-Cola is a favorite beverage at many meals, particularly at lunchtime, for those who can afford it.

Fast food is becoming a bigger part of Filipino culture, especially in larger cities, where chain restaurants abound. Most meals at such restaurants include

Jollibee is a popular fast-food restaurant based in the Philippines. Starting out as an ice cream parlor in 1975, it now has more than 600 locations in the Philippines and 30 locations worldwide.

There are more than 300 fruit and nut species native to the Philippines.

rice, but French fries are a clear favorite among teens. Banana ketchup, also known as banana sauce, is the condiment of choice. Banana ketchup has a similar consistency to tomato ketchup and is sometimes colored red.

For dinner, teens might sit down to a meal of fish, chicken, or pork served with a vegetable or mung bean soup. When it comes to pork, the fattier the better. Small cubes of browned pork fat that have been fried until crispy are a special treat.

Fruit Is a Favorite

The Philippines' tropical climate means fruits are plentiful. There are several varieties of bananas, including yellow, red, and green. The mango is the national fruit of the Philippines. The juicy orange-yellow fruit is found in a variety of favorite drinks and dishes. On special occasions, Filipinos prepare a fruit salad that combines the freshest fruits of the season with sweet, creamy condensed milk.

Durian is considered the king of all tropical fruit. A single fruit can grow to 10 pounds (4.5 kilograms). Covered in sharp spikes, durian is an expensive treat and can cost as much as 83 to 124 pesos (U.S.$2 to $3) per pound (0.45 kg). Famous for its pungent smell, some countries have banned the fruit in hotels, restaurants, and airports. A common saying among Filipinos is, "Durian is a fruit that smells like hell but tastes like heaven."

Chores Are a Chore

With so many Filipino teens in large families, there is a lot of work to be done. The average Filipino family has 3.5 children, compared with 2.09 in the United States and 2.5 in the world. Teens, usually older sisters, are asked to help care for younger siblings. Teens must feed and bathe them, change their clothes, and get them ready for school.

Domestic work is a considerable part of a Filipino woman's day. Urban women spend an average of six hours a day doing chores, while rural women average an additional half hour of work.

Fish is a staple food in the Philippines.

Young girls help their mothers with the laundry, dishes, cooking, and cleaning. Boys are asked to take out the garbage, gather firewood, or help their fathers with farm chores or household repairs.

Mealtime Means Rice Time

Whether it is with breakfast, lunch, or dinner, Filipinos do not consider a meal complete unless rice is served. Rice is one of the country's most abundant crops, and plain steamed rice is a staple of the Filipino diet. For most meals, the rice is cooked first because it takes longer than other foods. When it is ready, it is placed on the table to cool while other courses are made and served. Most Filipino meals are served cold or at room temperature.

None of the most common dishes are considered spicy. However, ginger, garlic, and peppers are common ingredients in Filipino meals because of their health benefits. Most tables also serve *patis*, a salty fish sauce.

Knife, Fork, Spoon? Not Necessarily

Spoons and forks are common at most Filipino meals, but they're not required. In some traditional meals, food is eaten on a banana leaf. In other cases, diners just use their hands. It is common to see Filipinos eating with their hands at a restaurant or at home. Both are normal methods throughout the country. Table knives are rarely—if ever—used.

27

Green beans and potatoes are standard dishes in Filipino meals. A common ingredient, used in soups and salads, are the leaves from the tops of *camote*, a sweet potato. *Ube* is a bright purple potato used in everything from cakes to ice cream. For dessert, *halo-halo* is a tasty treat. The word "halo" means "mix," and this popular dessert snack is a combination of shaved ice and milk mixed with ingredients like mung beans, ube, coconut milk, gelatin, ice cream, and rice.

Teens are often asked to help in the kitchen by chopping vegetables, setting the table, or clearing and washing dishes at the end of the meal.

patis
pah-TEES
camote
kah-MOH-ti
ube
OOH-bi
halo-halo
haloh-haloh

Getting Around

Getting around in the Philippines depends largely on where a person lives. In the cities, cars and fuel are very expensive, so only the wealthiest families have their own vehicles. Most teens and their families rely on buses, taxis, trains, and bicycles to go to school or work.

Filipinos can get a learning permit when they are 16, which allows them

Taxis, buses, Jeepneys, horsedrawn carriages, and motorcycles are all available to the passenger in need.

to drive if a licensed adult accompanies them. At 17, they can drive on their own. Professional drivers—those who drive for a living, like taxi or bus drivers—must be at least 18 years old.

In the country, teens often walk or ride bicycles. In remote and mountainous regions, they might rely on a horse-drawn cart or ride on a pack animal to get where they need to go.

Embracing New Technology

Filipinos—especially teens—have been quick to adopt new technology like computers, cell phones, and digital music. With one of the world's highest

The Jeepney

After World War II, as American troops who had occupied the Philippines began leaving, they left behind hundreds of military Jeeps. Filipinos modified the Jeeps, converting them into buses that could carry a dozen or more people. They decorated their creations with colorful paint, fluttering flags, and flashing lights. The vehicles became known as Jeepneys, most likely a combination of Jeep and *jitney*, which is a small bus found in many parts of the world. In rural areas of the Philippines where vehicles are scarce, Jeepneys can be seen with passengers crammed inside,

jitney
jit-nee

sitting on the roof, hanging off the sides, and even sitting on the hood.

The average Jeepney seats 16 passengers. A 2.5-mile (4-km) ride averages 7.5 pesos (U.S. 18 cents).

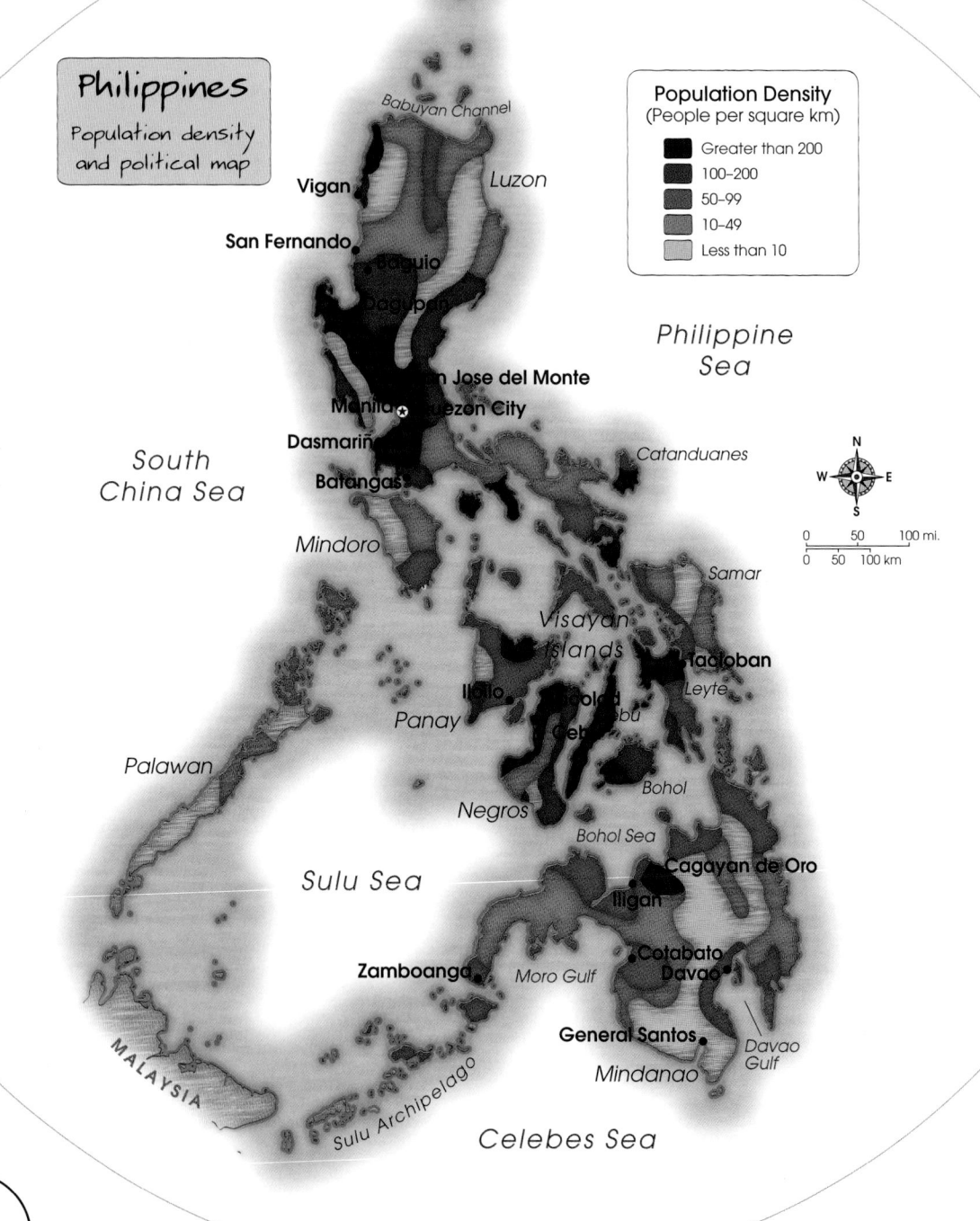

Philippines
Population density and political map

Population Density
(People per square km)

- Greater than 200
- 100–200
- 50–99
- 10–49
- Less than 10

Babuyan Channel

Luzon

Vigan

San Fernando

Baguio

Dagupan

Philippine Sea

San Jose del Monte

Manila Quezon City

Dasmariñ

Batangas

Mindoro

Catanduanes

N
W E
S

0   50   100 mi.
0   50   100 km

Samar

Visayan Islands

Tacloban

Iloilo

Bacolod

Leyte

Panay

Cebu

South China Sea

Palawan

Negros

Bohol

Bohol Sea

Sulu Sea

Cagayan de Oro

Iligan

Cotabato

Zamboanga

Moro Gulf

Davao

General Santos

Davao Gulf

MALAYSIA

Sulu Archipelago

Mindanao

Celebes Sea

percentages of cell phone users, more than 35 million Filipinos are mobile. Cellular technology often replaces land-based telephone lines. Like in the West, teens love using their cell phones to send text messages or pictures to their friends. In urban areas, teens are frequently seen playing handheld video games or listening to iPods.

Internet cafés are popular places for teens to connect with the rest of the world. There, they can surf their favorite Web sites, watch online videos, read their friends' blogs, send e-mails, or do homework. Most often, though, they visit chat rooms and send instant messages back and forth to friends.

Filipinos lead the world in cell phone texting, sending more than 50 million messages a day. In 2001, protesters organized rallies against President Joseph Estrada through texting. These protests helped force President Estrada's resignation.

Big City, Bustling Streets

Shoppers can get the best foods for the lowest prices from traditional market vendors.

Manila is the Philippines' largest metropolitan area. With more than 10 million residents, the city is home to around 12 percent of all Filipinos. It is the capital as well as the cultural, political, and entertainment center of the country.

Manila is almost always busy. Buses, taxicabs, and cars compete for space on the streets. Workers, shoppers, and students hustle along the sidewalks.

With its huge office and apartment buildings, Manila has a distinctly Western feel. In fact, Manila is so similar to big American cities that it is said to have a "Coca-Cola culture." Teens can eat at McDonald's, shop for Levi's jeans, watch the latest American blockbuster, play the hottest new video games, and listen to hit singles from American artists on their iPods.

Browsing and Buying at the Mall or Market

While modern malls and supermarkets are common in urban areas of the Philippines, traditional outdoor markets, called *palengkes*, continue to serve Filipino teens and their families. Weekends are popular times for young Filipinos to head to these markets. Merchants set up stalls under colorful canopies for protection from the sun and occasional rain showers. They offer fresh foods, including fruit, vegetables, fish, meat, poultry, eggs, and milk. Other vendors sell clothing, shoes, handicrafts, and art.

palengkes
pah-LAYNG-kays

Filipino Time, Not Always Timely

The markets are crowded with people haggling for the best prices. The barter system is still common here, and people trade goods and services with one another instead of using money. Jeepneys, pedicabs, and taxis wait to carry shoppers home with their supplies.

Household Help is Common

Middle- and upper-income families often rely on hired help for household chores. Because poverty continues to be a problem in many parts of the Philippines, household help is relatively cheap. Women are hired to do laundry, clean, cook, and grocery shop, and also look after and take care of young children. Men most often work as gardeners, drivers, or butlers.

A Filipino's sense of time does not necessarily follow the hands on the clock or the day on the calendar. Filipinos often joke about how they operate on "Filipino time." People may arrive hours late for social gatherings and still be "fashionably late." In rural areas, people may show up hours, or even days, late because of weather or problems with transportation. Even the airlines are said to run on Filipino time. The acronym for the Philippine Airlines, or PAL, is sometimes said to stand for "Plane Always Late."

Although the birth rate in the Philippines has halved (from six children to three) since the 1970s, poor families are still generally larger than others families by at least one member. Nearly 21 percent of poor families have seven family members or more. Only 6 percent of other families reach that size.

3

The More the Merrier

FOR MOST FILIPINOS, FAMILY COMES FIRST. That is why it is not uncommon for teens in the Philippines to live with their parents, grandparents, and maybe even aunts, uncles, and cousins. Extended Filipino families are so close-knit that cousins are often considered sisters and brothers, and nieces and nephews are treated like sons and daughters.

Sometimes three or four generations live together. They rely on one another to keep house, care for children, tend to the elderly, and help pay for household expenses.

There are very few nursing homes in the Philippines. The elderly are taken care of by their children and grandchildren. Usually one adult child—often a daughter—will continue caring for parents as they age. Even if she is married with her own family, it is expected that she will look after her parents until they die. Filipinos consider it their duty and honor to take care of their parents.

In some areas, houses are built on the same piece of land so an extended family can live together. The collection of homes can grow quite large, depending on the size of the property or farm that needs tending.

Filipino parents consider it their duty to provide for the material and educational needs of their children. In turn, Filipino children are expected to obey and respect their parents.

Family Size

Filipino parents usually have two or three children. But because of extended-family living arrangements, the size of their household is usually much larger. Rural areas have families with four, five, six, or more children who are asked to

help on the farm as they grow older.

Child-care duties are split between the mother and father. Dads carry, feed, and play with their children, but mothers are still called upon to change diapers. Since both parents are likely to have jobs, grandparents are the primary caregivers during the day. They look after the youngest children while their parents are away and welcome their older grandchildren home from school.

The Blessing of Parenthood

Until a child is born, a Filipino couple is not considered to be a family. The birth of a child is seen as God's blessing on the marriage. Although sons are often preferred, gender is not as important as it is in other Asian countries.

The arrival of a child gives parents added purpose and a reason to succeed. They work extra hard to support their children, paying for schooling, books, and clothes. Parents gladly go without things for themselves so their children can be happy and comfortable.

The children are also considered a reason for parents to stay committed to each other. Difficulties and differences

Earthquakes and the Ring of Fire

Part of daily life in the Philippines is experiencing the rumbling and shaking from earthquakes. The Philippines lies in an area called the Ring of Fire. The name comes from a circle of active volcanoes in the Pacific Ocean. Earthquakes are associated with some of the volcanic activity. The country experiences from five to 10 earthquake tremors a day. These quakes are usually more annoying than dangerous. Some are so small they are not felt at all, but some have been quite destructive.

In 1976, a powerful quake shook the island of Mindanao. The earthquake created a tsunami, which leveled buildings and killed more than 8,000 people. In 1990, a violent earthquake hit Luzon, toppling dozens of buildings and leaving more than 1,000 dead. Tougher construction standards have helped the Philippines guard against major earthquake damage. Schools conduct regular drills to keep students safe during quakes.

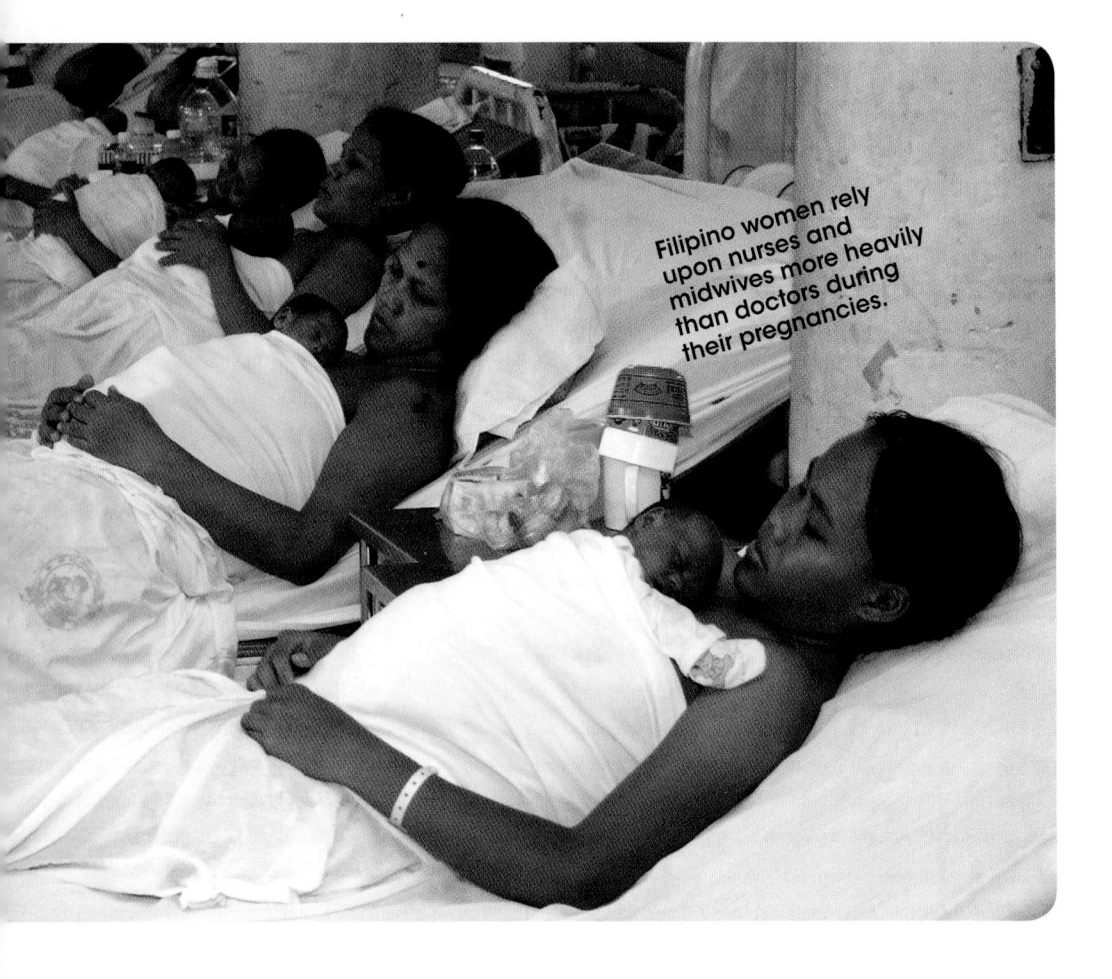

Filipino women rely upon nurses and midwives more heavily than doctors during their pregnancies.

that arise during their marriage are quickly smoothed over for the sake of the children.

Children are a blessing to Filipino families, and having many children is seen as a sign of a father's masculinity and a mother's womanhood. All couples expect and want to have children, and when they cannot, they often adopt the young child of a close relative.

Child-rearing in Advance

Even before a child is born, a Filipino family is closely involved in the coming event. Mothers who develop strange cravings for odd foods in the middle of the night are catered to by loving husbands. They believe the child is already beginning to form its personality and make its wishes known. If an expectant mother is easily bothered by her husband's behavior, she is thought

Most Popular Baby Names

Boys' Names	Girls' Names
Michael	Maricel
Ronald	Michelle
Ryan	Jennifer
Joseph	Janice
Joel	Mary Grace
Jeffrey	Jocelyn
Marlon	Catherine
Richard	Mary Anne
Noel	Rowena
Jonathan	Grace

to be carrying a child who will turn out to be like her husband.

Filipinos have several superstitions about children around the time of their birth. In rural areas, the placenta (the organ that holds the baby during pregnancy) is sometimes buried with certain objects or tossed into a stream.

If the placenta is buried with a pencil or newspaper, it is believed the child will be intelligent. If it goes into a stream, the child is considered likely to become a wanderer. While this is an infrequent practice, some families still believe these superstitions.

Most Filipino children are born into Roman Catholic families. Within

Although families may not have much money for activities, they value the time they do spend together.

a few months, Filipino babies are baptized in a ceremony at their family church. Family members and close friends are invited to the occasion. The parents announce their choice for the child's godparents at the ceremony.

Urban and Rural Homes

The type of homes in which Filipino teens live depends on where they live, how wealthy or poor their families are, and what the weather and geography are like. In big cities, tall, gleaming glass and steel apartment buildings dominate the skyline. High-rise apartment living is the norm, since building space is scarce. In the largest cities, roughly half of the families are poor. Parts of larger cities have tenement housing and shacks.

The picture is much different in rural areas, where poverty is even more common. Nearly 80 percent of the Philippines' rural population lives in poverty. Poorer rural families often live in nipa huts, which are made of bamboo with roofs of leaves or metal. In some areas, homes are made of discarded scraps of wood and metal. Such fragile houses are a large reason

Nipa huts have been called primitive by colonizers of the Philippines, but the building style continues to this day.

The Earliest Filipinos

There have been people living on the islands of the Philippines for thousands of years. Exactly how they got there is something of a mystery. The earliest people to arrive in the Philippines are believed to have walked across land bridges that were connected to what later became Malaysia and China. The first to arrive 25,000 years ago may have been short, dark-skinned hunter-gatherers. These people are believed to have migrated from mainland Asia. Later immigrants came from what today is Indonesia.

When the land bridges disappeared, people came by boat. They brought bronze and copper and built rice terraces, which are used to irrigate crops. They also introduced the *carabao*, a water buffalo used to help with farming.

By the beginning of the first century, residents of the Philippines were regularly trading with China. They exchanged metals and woods for finished Chinese products.

carabao
kah-rah-BOWE

typhoons can be so devastating. The flimsy dwellings provide little safety from strong winds and heavy rains. In 2006, Typhoon Durian killed more than 700 people in the Philippines.

Farming and Fishing Are the Old Ways of Life

It is a hot and humid April afternoon on the island of Samar in the Visayas chain of islands in the Philippines. A teen boy is helping his father harvest rice in the family's rice paddies. Down a dusty dirt road at a neighboring farm, the boy's best friend is helping his family work in the cornfields.

Roughly 40 percent of Filipino families support themselves by farming. Yet the country struggles to grow enough rice to feed its growing population.

The rice terraces in northern Luzon are thought of as one of the wonders of the world and have been called "stairways to heaven."

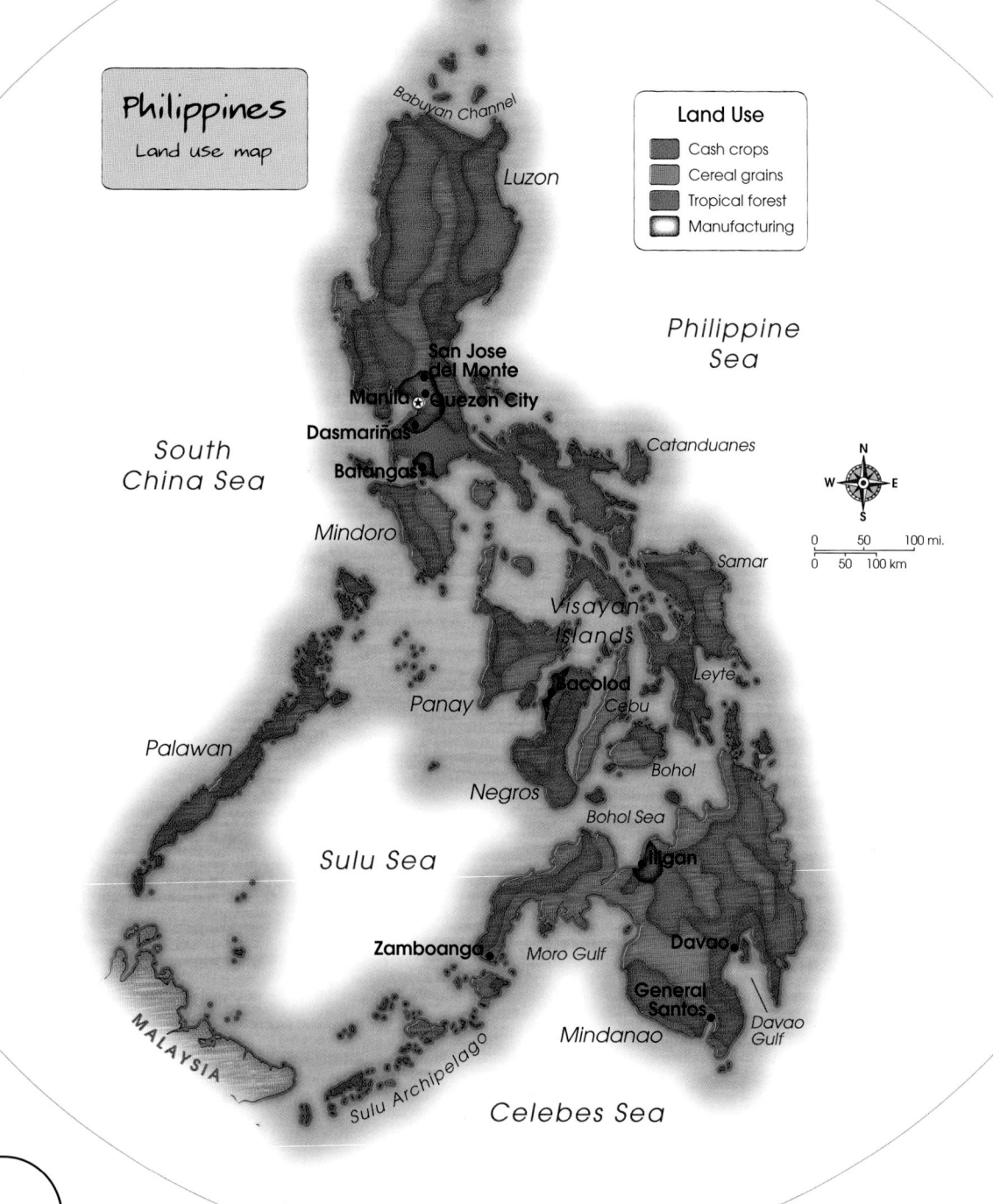

Philippines
Land use map

Land Use
- Cash crops
- Cereal grains
- Tropical forest
- Manufacturing

Babuyan Channel

Luzon

Philippine Sea

San Jose del Monte
Manila · Quezon City
Dasmariñas
Batangas
Catanduanes

South China Sea

Mindoro

Samar

Visayan Islands

Bacolod
Cebu
Leyte

Panay

Bohol

Palawan

Negros

Bohol Sea

Iligan

Sulu Sea

Zamboanga
Moro Gulf
Davao

MALAYSIA

General Santos
Mindanao
Davao Gulf

Sulu Archipelago

Celebes Sea

N
W · E
S

0   50   100 mi.
0   50   100 km

In 2006, Filipino farmers produced about 15 million tons (13.5 million metric tons) of rice. Another 1.65 million tons (1.5 metric tons) was imported. Still, the number of mouths to feed is increasing. In 2007, it was estimated that the population's birth rate was nearly five times that of the death rate.

Except for a short time in the 1970s, the Philippines has not grown enough rice to feed its population since 1903. However, government agricultural experts predict that by 2010, new farming techniques and technology will allow the country to grow enough rice for its people.

Hanging Out, Arm-in-Arm

A Filipino teen and her best friend walk arm-in-arm down the street. Her mother and a family friend follow behind. Later that evening, her father takes a stroll with his best friend, and their arms are also interlocked.

Filipinos are fond of taking walks together, and they often hold hands or stroll arm-in-arm as they talk. It doesn't matter whether companions are the same sex. This touching is a symbol of mutual affection, friendship, and support.

Teens in urban areas are often spotted chatting with their friends at

Filipino teens are not shy about touching in public.

45

shopping malls, town plazas, fast-food restaurants, museums, and sporting events. They talk about their favorite music, TV shows, and fashion styles, or gossip about who is dating whom. They may gather at a friend's house to watch a movie or head out to a karaoke lounge to sing their favorite pop star's latest hit.

In rural areas, pastimes for teens vary with the seasons. Some communities have frequent festivals or fairs. Other areas have picnics with games and prizes. During the rainy season, teens spend more time indoors listening to the radio, reading, or taking in a bit of Filipino folklore from a grandparent or other older relative.

Dating in Groups, Then as Couples

In cities, a friend of the same sex is called a *barkada*. Teens hang out with their barkadas until they are old enough to marry. The first steps toward dating begin when teens are 13 or 14, when boys and girls meet in groups with their

barkada
bar-KAH-dah

Building Styles Are Still Spanish

Because Spain controlled the Philippines for centuries, many buildings in the islands have a distinctly Spanish style. Homes are usually made of split or woven bamboo, wood, or hollow blocks made from concrete. To deflect the intense heat of the midday sun, they are often painted white. Roofs are sometimes covered with red clay tiles for the same reason. Summer temperatures in the Philippines can reach 104 degrees Fahrenheit (40 degrees Celsius).

Many homes are surrounded by ornate, wrought-iron gates and fences that enclose small yards and neatly manicured gardens. Large brick churches are the focal points of many Filipino towns. Built during the period of Spanish colonial rule, the churches remain central gathering places for many families.

In 2007, more than 6,000 couples attended the annual kissing festival called "Lovapalooza" in Manila. The festival broke a Guinness world record for number of couples kissing at the same time.

friends. The mixed group may go to the mall, the video arcade, or the movies. By the time teens are 16 or 17, they might begin dating as couples and going to concerts and dance clubs. It is not considered proper for young couples to kiss on the first date, but they might hold hands or walk arm-in-arm.

Many Filipino teens do not have to choose between spending time with friends or with their families. Sometimes it is the same group of people. Many have large families with siblings and cousins close to their own age whom they consider friends.

More than 10,000 dancers and musicians gather annually to celebrate Sinulog, the largest religious festival in the country.

4

Party Again and Again

WITH SEEMINGLY COUNTLESS LOCAL FESTIVALS, NATIONAL AND RELIGIOUS HOLIDAYS, BIRTHDAYS, WEDDINGS, AND BAPTISMS, FILIPINOS ARE ALWAYS HAVING A PARTY. When they get together with family and friends, the groups are often big and hungry, making food a central component.

When a young Filipino celebrates a birthday, the party combines traditional Filipino themes with newer Western elements. There is usually a big, colorful birthday cake, balloons, and presents. There are also piñatas and dishes of long noodles, which symbolize a long life. Outside, colorful lights and decorations signal the event. Early in the day, the family attends Mass to thank God for the blessing of the child.

Weddings With a Cast of Dozens

Young Filipinos start to look for spouses by their early 20s. Women usually marry between the ages of 20 and 25, while men marry from 25 to 30. Some young professionals wait even longer. It is not uncommon for Filipinos to have engagements of seven years or longer while they finish their studies.

Arranged marriages, when parents pick a spouse for their child, are not common in Filipino culture. However, it is customary for a man to ask the parents of his bride-to-be for permission to marry their daughter. This occasion is marked by a formal ceremony called a *pamanhikan*. If the woman's parents consent, the man's parents will traditionally pay for the couple's wedding.

pamanhikan
pah-manh-HEE-kahn

A Special Bond With Godparents

The tradition of Filipino parents' choosing godparents for their children began when the Philippines was under Spanish rule. The tradition has only grown. Today some children can have eight or more sets of godparents.

Godparents are considered second parents to the child, and they share a lifelong bond. A godfather is called *ninong*, and a godmother is called *ninang*. The godparents are expected to look after the child, should anything happen to the parents. They give special gifts on Christmas and birthdays and are expected to help their godchild find a job or otherwise get a good start in life.

Godparents become closely tied to the parents of the child, and the four are considered *compadres* and *comadres*, or close friends, even though they might not have known each other before the baptism. The importance of the occasion can be measured by the godparents' prominence. Public officials are popular choices as godparents, and some have hundreds or even thousands of godchildren.

ninong
nee-nong
ninang
nee-nang
compadres
kohm-PAH-drays
comadres
koh-MAH-drays

Holidays

People Power Day—February 25

Maundy Thursday—March or April

Good Friday—Day after Maundy Thursday

Easter—March or April

Araw ng Kagitingan (Bataan Day)—April 9

Labor Day—May 1

Independence Day—June 12

Ninoy Aquino Day—August 21

National Heroes Day—Last Sunday in August

All Saints Day—November 1

End of Ramadan—varies depending on Islamic calendar

Bonifacio Day—November 30

Christmas Day—December 25

Rizal Day—December 30

New Year's Eve—December 31

If a Filipino male is not married by his late 20s, his female relatives may begin playing matchmaker. They seek suitable mates among their friends and co-workers and arrange for the two to go on dates.

Many Filipino weddings involve two ceremonies. The first is a legal ceremony in a city office. A more elaborate, religious ceremony takes place later in a church.

Dozens of people take part in a typical wedding. The bride and groom are joined by their best man and maid of honor, along with bridesmaids and

Party Time Means Mealtime

Food is a central ingredient in most Filipino holiday celebrations, festivals, and parties. Tables are piled high with rice, meat, and fresh seafood.

Léchon is served at most special Filipino occasions. Léchon *baboy* is a pig or piglet, and léchon *baka* is a cow or calf. Both are roasted for hours over hot coals until the skin turns crispy. The fatty insides are sliced and served, and strips of skin attached to fat are the most prized pieces. A léchon baboy can weigh between 18 and 132 pounds (8 and 60 kg) and can cost anywhere from 2,500 to 8,000 pesos (U.S.$60 to $193). One léchon storeowner said:

If you have léchon at your party, you're "big time." When someone says, "We will have a léchon for you," it means you're an important guest.

Dog meat is also considered a delicacy to some Filipinos. However, it is no longer sold in markets because of concerns about rabies, a disease that can be contracted by eating the brain.

Special occasions mean special beverages. For men, it is usually gin or beer served with a *balut*, a duck egg containing an embryo. Women enjoy beer, wine, gin, rum, or *tuba*, a coconut wine popular in regions where coconut trees are abundant. Children and teens favor soft drinks, coconut milk, or fruit juice.

A popular dessert at ceremonial meals is sticky rice. To make it, a special rice dish is cooked with coconut milk and sugarcane syrup and wrapped in banana leaves.

léchon
LIT-son
baboy
BAH-boy
baka
BAH-kah
balut
bah-LOOT
tuba
TOO-bah

Guests gauge the importance of the host and the ceremony by the amount of léchon served.

groomsmen. Also attending are sponsors, friends, and relatives who hold high status in their community. Sponsors are expected to give the couple money to help pay for the wedding and give them a head start. The number of sponsors depends on how successful a couple is expected to be. The more sponsors they have, the more likely they are to be well educated and have a wealthy family. At some weddings, money is pinned to the clothes of the bride and groom to help their marriage start successfully.

Many Filipino weddings are followed by a big feast, with the bride and groom sitting at the front of the room. Nearby a white paper cage hangs with two long silk ribbons under it. Inside the cage, two white doves await the moment when the bride and groom will pull the ribbons and release them. The doves symbolize the bride and groom leaving to start their new life together. The birds flutter about the room and cause a bit of a disruption until they are captured.

The bride and groom cut the wedding cake together, and at some weddings, the unmarried female guests are given a small wrapped present with their "fortune" inside.

Most Filipino couples stay together for life. Under Filipino law, divorce does not exist.

Gathering to Grieve

Filipinos rally their families for births, baptisms, and weddings. It is no different when it comes to deaths and funerals. They gather as soon as a loved one has died, holding vigil over the

The First House

It is common for newlyweds to live with the bride's or groom's parents for the first year. They use the time to get settled and figure out where they want to live and work. When they finally move into a home of their own, sometimes on the family's property, it is an important beginning marked by a house blessing and housewarming party. Filipinos believe it is not proper to live in a house without first blessing it. Also important is throwing a party with friends and family who wish the young couple happiness and prosperity.

The religious ceremony includes many prayers. A priest sprinkles holy water throughout the house. An elder might also toss a shower of coins for luck, while prominent guests carry lighted candles. In rural areas, rice is the first item carried inside a new house. This action will symbolize the hope that the family always has enough food.

If a house has been built especially for the young couple, there are several traditions. A silver coin is placed inside each of the main support posts as a symbol of good fortune. Also during construction, the owner counts the steps leading into the house. If the number can be divided by three, it is considered bad luck. The owner walks up the stairs chanting *Oro, plata, mata*, which means "Gold, silver, death." If the chant ends with mata, or death, a step is added or subtracted.

Oro, plata, mata
or-oh, plah-tah, mah-tah

In the past, rich families hired people to live in cemeteries to maintain crypts and prevent vandalism. However, poverty has forced the poor to get creative when it comes to finding a place to live, and today more than 10,000 people call the cemetery in Manila home.

body day and night. They take turns keeping watch for as long as three days, until the funeral. Friends and relatives send flowers and prayer cards to the family of the deceased. Those facing financial problems might also receive money to help cover funeral expenses.

A Filipino funeral is usually not a quiet affair. There is often loud weeping. Widows wear a black dress and veil, while men dress in black pants and a white shirt with a black armband. Yet despite the sadness of the occasion, Filipinos work hard to accommodate their guests with an elaborate spread of food and beverages.

In rural areas, funeral ceremonies may include domino or card games and riddle contests so those holding vigil over the deceased can stay awake. In small towns and in the country, the dead are usually buried in the town

Families who cannot afford a proper funeral sometimes raise money by holding card games, with the proceeds going toward the burial.

cemetery. In cities, many families have large mausoleums where the remains are placed in vaults in the walls.

For Filipinos, the mourning does not stop with the burial. A year after the deceased has been buried, families gather again to mark the occasion with a death anniversary. They attend a special Mass, visit graves, or hold a memorial service.

Making the Most of Holidays

More than 80 percent of Filipinos are Catholic, and religious holidays dominate the calendar. Easter is by far the biggest religious event in the Philippines. In Christian parts of the country, offices, schools, shops, and restaurants are closed for Maundy Thursday and Good Friday in the week before Easter. Teens and their families gather to pray, attend church, or watch an Easter parade near their home.

First Communion, a Milestone

Since most Filipinos are Catholic, the rite of first communion is a treasured event for most girls and boys. They are generally around 7 or 8 years old when they first receive the holy sacrament, which is usually a cracker or wafer and some wine. These represent the body and blood of Jesus Christ. Boys may wear a white shirt and dark pants, while girls wear a special white dress and veil. The ceremony is followed by a big party with friends and family.

Another coming-of-age tradition for boys between the ages of 10 and 14 is circumcision, which is the removal of the foreskin of the penis. In larger cities, the procedure is usually performed just after a boy is born. In rural areas

though, teenage circumcision remains common. A boy goes with friends to a barber or somebody else who does the job. Having the procedure done is the boy's choice, and it usually is not mentioned to the rest of the family.

Girls Debut at 18

When a Filipino girl turns 18, she can make her debut as a young woman. At that age, she is considered ready for marriage and entrance into the adult world. The event calls for a big party

Easter is the biggest holiday in the Philippines, surpassing even Christmas. The Philippines is the only officially Catholic country in Asia.

Rizal Day

Every December 30, Filipino teens and their families gather to celebrate Rizal Day. The holiday marks the death of the Philippines' national hero, José Rizal. Rizal was a patriot and revolutionary who opposed Spain's occupation of the Philippines. Born the seventh of 11 children of a middle-class family, Rizal was a strong student who graduated from college at 16. He was a gifted mathematician, eye doctor, playwright, novelist, inventor, and artist who spoke 22 languages. He argued in his books and speeches that the Philippines should be an independent nation, free from Spain's influence.

Spain controlled the Philippines for more than 300 years. Rizal felt the country had established itself long before Spain took control. He founded La Liga Filipina, a progressive organization aimed at giving Filipinos a better life and protecting them against "all violence and injustice." The group made government officials uncomfortable, and Rizal was arrested as an enemy of the state.

On December 30, 1896, Rizal was executed by a firing squad, but not before he could write one last poem. Titled *My Last Farewell*, Rizal's words further moved those opposed to Spanish rule into action.

Rizal was secretly buried in an unmarked grave, and a monument was built where he was shot. The rebellion against Spain continued for two years after Rizal's death. Today there are many reminders of his contribution to the modern, independent Philippines. Monuments to him stand in just about every town plaza in the country, and his face is on the one-peso coin.

Religions in the Philippines

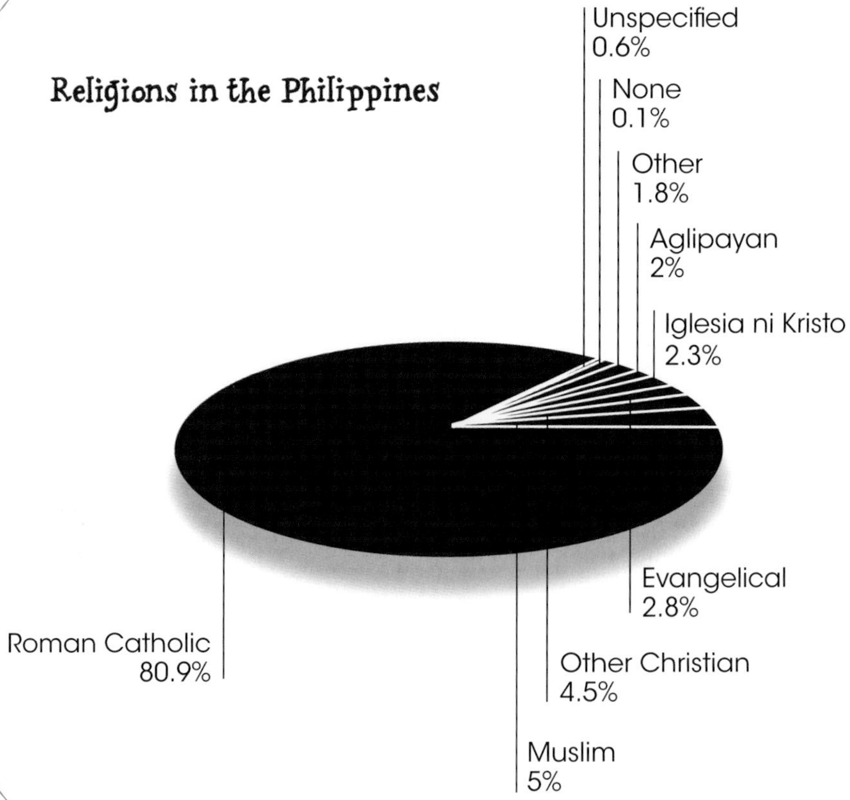

Unspecified
0.6%

None
0.1%

Other
1.8%

Aglipayan
2%

Iglesia ni Kristo
2.3%

Evangelical
2.8%

Other Christian
4.5%

Muslim
5%

Roman Catholic
80.9%

Source: United States Central Intelligence Agency
The World Factbook—The Philippines

and a dance, with all of her friends and relatives in attendance. These formal parties are called *cotillons*.

Young, single guests are encouraged to bring dates to the debut dance. Teens wear formal clothes, and young males give their dates a corsage.

For wealthier families, the occasion is an opportunity to put on a huge affair with lavish gifts, music, and catered buffets. Some families spend weeks rehearsing for the cotillon. It is seen as a huge honor to be invited to dance.

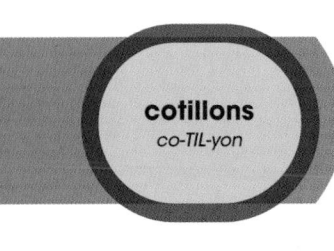

cotillons
co-TIL-yon

Selling fireworks is a quick way to make money in the Philippines—superstitious Filipinos believe that noisy New Year's celebrations drive away evil spirits.

5

On The Job

CHILDREN UNDER 15 ARE NOT ALLOWED TO WORK OUTSIDE THEIR HOMES. Those between 15 and 18 can hold part-time jobs, but their hours are restricted, and the work cannot be dangerous.

In cities, teens often work in fast-food restaurants, retail shops, or movie theaters. Girls might baby-sit for a friend or neighbor for a few extra pesos. A boy might earn spending money doing odd jobs such as mowing lawns or washing cars. Many rural children under 15 are asked to work on the family farm. They help harvest rice and other crops or tend to animals.

Young and Unemployed

Nearly half of the unemployed workers are between 15 and 24. The unemployment rate for this age group is 21 percent, more than two and a half times the rate for the rest of the population. Such numbers are discouraging for many young people. In a recent survey, about 44 percent of young Filipinos said they worried they would never find a job. However, employment rates, especially among young women, seem to be rising. Increased enrollment in school is helping more young people get the skills they need to enter the work force.

The fast-food industry is a popular place for teens to start their working career. Jollibee alone has more than 26,000 employees. Other restaurants are opening all the time, including SPAM Jam, a restaurant specializing in food made of SPAM.

Work Hours and Wages Vary

Laws regulating the number of hours Filipinos work are loosely enforced. The government sets the workweek at 48 hours and the workday at eight hours. That leaves one day of rest per week, but many workers log many more than 48 hours a week, and some have more than one job.

Women, on average, work more than men. The average Filipino woman works 41.3 hours a week, compared with 40.4 hours for a man. Women are three times as likely as a man to work more than 64 hours a week. The longer workweek for women is due to a rapid growth in service industry jobs, positions that are largely filled by women.

Despite the number of hours, Filipinos usually work at a casual and leisurely pace. Hourly workers have required lunch and rest periods. Office workers sometimes have long lunch meetings that can stretch two or three hours, with many plates of food and glasses of drinks.

Pay rates vary widely in a country with such a large gap between rich and poor. The average annual income in 2006 was 172,000 pesos (U.S.$4,155). However, the actual pay range is huge. The poorest families made only 32,000 pesos (U.S.$773), while the richest families made 617,000 pesos (U.S.$14,900). The minimum wage also depends

on whether a job is in a big city or a remote village. For workers in the central part of the country near big cities like Manila, the minimum daily pay is 362 pesos (U.S.$8.75). But for those in the southernmost part of the country, the rate is only 180 pesos (U.S.$4.35) per day. Overtime pay must be given for work done beyond an eight-hour day or 48-hour week, with the rate depending on whether the overtime workday is a holiday.

Employers are not required to give employees paid vacation or paid sick leave. However, larger companies and

The United States is the Philippines' biggest market for exported goods, and is home to millions of Filipino immigrants. The Philippines is also the biggest exporter of labor in the world; contract workers are employed in places like Hong Kong, Singapore, and the Middle East.

corporations do give full-time workers paid vacations. Their length depends on how long the employee has been with the company. Many employees of small businesses do not enjoy these luxuries.

Different Sexes, Different Roles

The type of work teens will do when they grow up and enter the full-time work force depends on whether they are male or female. Jobs that require a lot of physical effort, like construction work, are generally held by men. Women are more likely to be employed as clerks or teachers, or in offices.

Young Filipino women are breaking down traditional barriers by staying in school longer. As they continue their education, they are becoming doctors and lawyers and filling jobs that traditionally have been held by men.

Yes Means Yes, No, or Maybe

For the most part, Filipinos are eager to please, and teens are no different. That becomes clear when they are asked to do a favor. Usually the answer is yes, but the real meaning may be yes, no, maybe, I don't know, or if it makes you happy.

Because of this ambiguity, invitations to dinner, a date, or a meeting are often

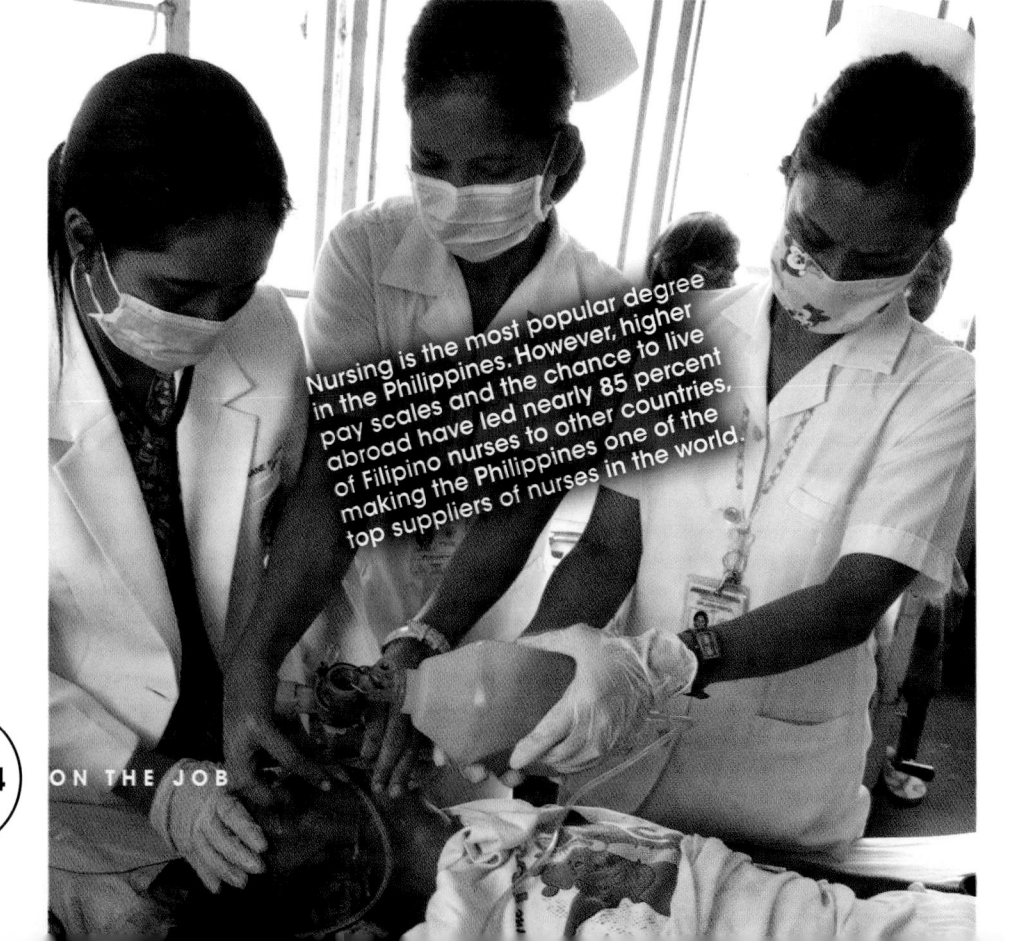

Nursing is the most popular degree in the Philippines. However, higher pay scales and the chance to live abroad have led nearly 85 percent of Filipino nurses to other countries, making the Philippines one of the top suppliers of nurses in the world.

confirmed and reconfirmed several times. Filipinos hate to say no, so they might say yes at first but later dodge the question or change the subject.

Commuting and the Workplace

In the largest cities, getting to and from work can feel like work itself. Traffic is snarled during the morning and evening rush hours, buses are often crowded, and motorcycles weave around Jeepneys, cars, and taxis competing for space.

When an office worker finally reaches his or her destination, the workplace is likely to have most of the modern comforts found in other

Amor Propio and Hiya

A teenage boy walks down the street carrying a large bag of groceries for his mother. He gets distracted while goofing around with his brother, trips, and falls, spilling the groceries and breaking some eggs. Other people see the boy's mistake, and his mother is naturally upset. Strangers smile politely or pretend not to see as his mother quietly helps him pick up the mess. She chooses not to scold him on the street. Instead, she talks to him privately about his mistake. She waits until later because of Filipinos' ideas about *amor propio* and *hiya*.

Amor propio means self-esteem; hiya means shame. Filipinos are raised to have a strong sense of self-esteem. If the mother had scolded her son in public, she would have risked damaging his self-esteem and causing him hiya. Such concern and consideration are common in the Philippines, particularly in the workplace. Co-workers are as likely as friends and family to respect other people's self-esteem. Even supervisors are careful not to scold employees in front of others, no matter how serious the offense. Throughout the country, it is considered rude to shame someone.

amor propio
ah-MORE PRO-pee-oh
hiya
HI-yah

Fish and other seafood provide more than half of all protein consumed by the average Filipino family.

major cities throughout the world. The question is whether those systems will be working properly. Frequent power failures shut down buildings' air conditioning, computers, and telephones, and disrupt the day's work. Filipinos take such hurdles in stride, shrug, and, of course, smile.

Economy Follows the Three Fs

Fishing, farming, and forestry account for around one-fifth of the 30 million jobs in the Philippines. The other occupations are largely spread among light manufacturing, mining, construction, and the service industry. The service industry includes everything from transportation to hotel and motel work,

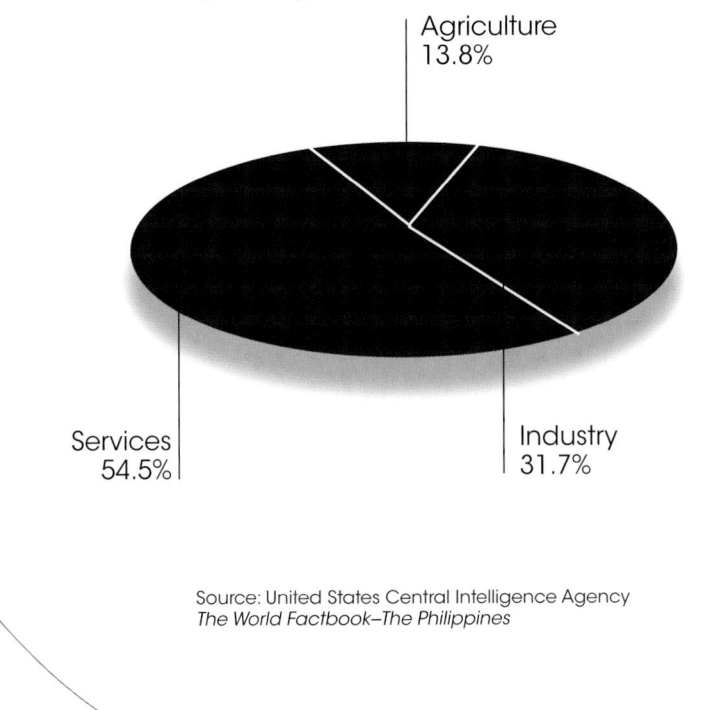

Labor Force by Occupation

Agriculture
13.8%

Services
54.5%

Industry
31.7%

Source: United States Central Intelligence Agency
The World Factbook–The Philippines

housekeeping, and gardening.

The unemployment rate is nearly 8 percent, and about 40 percent of the population lives below the government's poverty line. Since jobs and decent wages are often hard to come by, some people even volunteer to work without pay in the hope that it will one day lead to a regular paycheck.

Parents with children might work seven days a week and hold two or three jobs to support their family or to send their children to private school. Laws control the number of working hours and require safe working conditions. However, poorer and less educated workers risk being treated unfairly because employers can often find a replacement who will not complain.

Food Out, Fuel In

Just over a quarter of the land in the Philippines is suitable for farming. It is used to grow rice, bananas, cashews, pineapple, mangoes, and coconuts, all of which are often exported to

As farming rice becomes more expensive, farmers are faced with continued poverty or the pressure to sell their land to developers.

neighboring countries.

The Philippines' mountainous landscape makes it expensive to explore for minerals and fossil fuels. So most of the country's gas, oil, and iron is imported from other countries.

Filipinos, particularly those in remote areas, rely on locally grown food and goods. Imported items cost more because of the time, effort, and energy it takes to deliver them. The country's highway system is still developing. While shipping products between islands remains expensive, the government is working on ways to decrease the overall cost.

Skin Color Can Affect Status

While most Filipinos will agree that education is the key to achieving success, many associate a person's skin color with their ability. This belief dates back to colonial times, when white skin was highly valued. Some still think the shade of people's skin determines their success in the workplace and in society. One Filipino wrote:

... the influence of Western culture (Spain and the United States) caused her [my mother] to see Western beauty as the only true beauty. ... Especially with the older adults, the lighter you are, the better off you are; the darker you are, the worse you are. They categorize people's social standing through skin color.

Those with lighter skin are sometimes seen by others as better at their jobs and more intelligent overall.

A worker with light skin is likely to advance further at work than someone with a darker complexion, even if they have the same education and job skills.

Other factors that affect social status in the Philippines are money and financial success, political connections, family ties, and the importance of sponsors at weddings and baptisms. Those who are well connected are more likely to be promoted than their less well connected but perhaps more qualified co-workers.

Decisions, Decisions

If a Filipino business owner or executive is approached about a possible investment or other opportunity, he or she rarely gives an immediate yes or no answer. Often there are behind-the-scenes discussions and negotiations well before a meeting takes place. The business owner or executive is usually approached by a go-between who presents the proposal on behalf of the person seeking the approval.

While the owner or executive may consult with other board members or close associates, the final decision rests with him or her alone. Even if the opportunity makes perfect business sense, the person who makes the request is just as important. If the person is politically well connected and powerful, the idea is more likely to be accepted, regardless of how good it is.

From swimming to watching TV to hanging out with friends, teens in the Philippines never come up short with things to do.

6

Some Work, Some Play

AS HARD AS FILIPINOS WORK, THEY ALSO ENJOY THEIR LEISURE TIME. They spend vacations at home or away, but almost always with family. Filipinos share a passionate love of travel. Those who can afford it eagerly hop from island to island in their own country or jump on a plane and fly halfway around the world.

Vacations are often spent at beaches along the coast to escape the intense heat of May and June. The long stretch of cloudy, dark, wet days during the monsoon season from July through September are also spent vacationing.

For some families, there are expensive resorts with fancy rooms, pools, and restaurants. For others, a beach vacation might merely be a few days picnicking or playing games on the nearest beach. They might also use their time off to return to their hometowns to visit their family and friends.

The most popular destinations are those with lower temperatures, such as Baguio in the north or the hills of Tagaytay, which overlook a volcanic crater. Provinces like Cebu and historic towns in Ilocos and Vigan are also favorite spots to spend time away from home and work.

Sea kayaking, snorkeling, mountain biking, rock climbing, surfing, sailing, and hiking are only a few activities available to vacationing teens.

TV, Always a Teen Favorite

The comedy show *Bubble Gang* is popular among teens. For more than a decade, the television show's young actors and actresses have kept people laughing with their spoofs of commercials, politicians, and current events.

Other favorites include Filipino versions of American hit shows, including *Pinoy Big Brother*, where contestants live in front of cameras while trying not to get kicked out by their housemates. Another often-watched show is the sci-fi adventure series *Zaido: Pulis Pangkalawakan*, which features three young men battling evil throughout the galaxy. Teens also enjoy

The show *Wowowee* has made several world stops in the United States and Australia.

Myx Daily Top 10, a music program that airs videos of the day's most requested pop songs.

Few TV stars are bigger than Willie Revillame and his back-up dancers who are hosts of a midday game show called *Wowowee.* In 2006, a stampede of would-be contestants eager for five seconds of fame killed more than 70 fans of the show. Another top star is Kris Aquino. A popular product endorser and host of several TV shows, Aquino is the daughter of former president Corazon Aquino.

What They're Listening To

The Philippines has some of Asia's biggest popular music fans, and teens are some of the country's most enthusiastic admirers of pop stars. Other

So You Think You Can Sing?

A girl jumps on stage, grabs a microphone, and begins belting out her favorite Jennifer Lopez song. The singing is awful, but the girl is trying hard, and her friends laugh and cheer her on.

When teens really want to unwind, they head to the nearest club with karaoke—or videoke, as it is known in the Philippines. TV monitors show the words to songs, and a sound system carries the tune as singers do their best imitations of their favorite pop stars. Videoke is so popular, in fact, and audiences are so encouraging, that singers rarely show embarrassment or bashfulness. While some of the singing is truly awful, it is considered rude to tease a videoke performer, no matter how untalented.

Videoke booths can be found in nearly every club in every city.

favorite genres for teens are rap, hard rock, heavy metal, and music that combines contemporary sounds and styles with more traditional Filipino instruments and folk tunes. Many Filipino singers sing in Filipino or Taglish, mixing English with their native language. Latin American rhythms and melodies also have a strong presence in Filipino pop music.

Favorite Filipino performers include Urbandub, an experimental indie rock group; Moonstar 88, a female-fronted rock band; Kitchie Nadal, a female singer-songwriter and former lead singer of the group Mojofly; and Hale, a band famous for its aching love ballads.

Filipino teens enjoy making music as much as listening to it. One girl said:

Almost every teenager in the Philippines is knowledgeable in playing the guitar. I play three instruments—the guitar, the piano, and the bamboo flute, and I also love to sing. … Even prom nights turn out to be "concert nights." … Indeed, Filipino teenagers are productive, yet they also know how to have fun.

Filipinos Love Their Films

Pick any Friday or Saturday night in any city or town in the Philippines with a movie theater. Chances are it is probably packed with excited teens watching the latest flick. Filipinos—teens especially—are known for their love of cinema. Many of Manila's towering shopping malls boast multi-screen movie theaters.

While Hollywood movies are among the most popular with teens, the Filipino film industry is one of the world's most productive. Around 130 feature-length Filipino films are produced each year. One of the most popular actors among young people is Diether Ocampo, a male heartthrob who jumped from TV to movies with hits like *Soltera*, *Calvento Files*, and *G-mik: The Movie*.

Enjoying the Outdoors

After school, many kids race outdoors to play their favorite games. Young children might chase each other in a raucous game of tag known as *agawang sulok*. The person who is "it" tries to tag other players and secure a base. Older children might be standing in a circle, testing their skills at *sipa*. Colorful ribbons are tied to round pieces of metal or tin or rattan balls, and players see who can kick it and keep it in the air the greatest number of times.

agawang sulok
ah-GAH-wahng SU-luk
sipa
SEE-pah

Basketball is one of the Philippines' leading sports. Courts are found in just about every school yard and neighborhood playground. Teens play casual games after school and practice their dribbling and shooting skills.

Their love of basketball extends beyond playing it. The Philippines has

The volleyball offensive styles "set" and "spike" were invented in the Philippines in 1916.

professional basketball leagues. Former player Robert Jaworski of the Philippine Basketball Association is the country's best-known and most talented star. Watching the U.S. National Basketball Association games is also a favorite activity among teens.

Baseball, volleyball, and soccer are other leading team sports in Filipino high schools. Boys and girls play such sports together casually, but formal athletics are divided into boy and girl squads.

It's Spider-Fighting Time

In the Filipino countryside, teens scour jungles, fields, back alleys, and storage rooms in search of their next spider-fighting champ. They store their ferocious arachnids in boxes and feed them special foods to get them ready for their next match.

Spider fights are held on a "death stick," a slim but sturdy twig or branch where the two battling spiders are placed. They fight back and forth, knocking one another off the stick. Children pull on their slender webs to put them back on the stick until one spider wraps the other in a web and is declared the victor. Children—and even some adults—sometimes bet on the spider they think will emerge as champion.

Though cockfighting is considered cruel in some cultures, it remains a popular pastime for teens and adults throughout the Philippines. Owners of gamecocks, or fighting roosters, raise

A fully-trained "battle cock" can fetch a price of more than 18,400 pesos (U.S. $445).

prized roosters who are put in a ring to do battle. The territorial roosters peck and claw at each other until one runs away or can no longer fight. The matches attract loud and excited crowds that cheer and bet on their favorite contestants.

Traditional Spectator Sports

In addition to taking in basketball games and soccer matches, Filipino teens and their families frequently attend local jai-alai, sipa, and *arnis de mano* matches. These are sports and activities that have been played throughout the country's history.

In jai alai, players use long wicker scoops to throw a small ball at high speeds in a three-walled court.

arnis de mano
ARR-nihs di MAH-noh

Put on Your Dancing Shoes

The Philippines' many festivals and celebrations often include dancing, and teenagers are some of the most active and enthusiastic participants. Dances are also part of town fiestas and school functions.

A boy who is interested in a girl might ask her to dance, but she is not likely to say yes right away. Instead, she might ask her friends, an older sibling, or a chaperone whether she should accept the invitation.

If she accepts, the two dance at almost arm's length from each other. The girl is upright and stiff, and the boy's arm can barely reach her waist. They might exchange a few words, but they rarely appear to be enjoying each other's company. If the music is fast, the couple may move quickly around the dance floor, but the girl will continue to look shy and bashful. When the song is over, she offers the boy a quick thanks and hurries back to her seat, most likely to chat with her friends about the experience. This display of indifference prevents both the boy and girl from feeling ashamed if their attraction is unreturned.

Dancing with a group of friends or siblings is a completely different experience. These teens are more likely to bounce around the dance floor, laughing and smiling and showing not a trace of the nervousness they had dancing in pairs.

The game was brought to the Philippines from Spain.

The spectator version of sipa, unlike the hacky-sacklike game that children play, resembles tennis without a racket. Players use their knees and feet to send a woven rattan ball called a shuttlecock back and forth over a net.

Arnis de mano, which means "harness of the hands," is an ancient form of martial arts. Contestants engage in hand-to-hand combat and wrestling and use special sticks in battles that resemble fencing or sword fighting.

Western Culture is Pop Culture

Many Filipinos, especially those in wealthier areas, embrace American culture. They love American foods, clothing, and music. The wealthier a family is, the more their lifestyle tends to reflect Western culture. Well-to-do Filipinos pride themselves on the number of Western friends they have. Instead of traditional wooden chairs and benches, wealthy Filipinos fill their homes with upholstered furniture. They collect the latest appliances and electronic gadgets and clothe their children in vast—and often expensive—wardrobes.

Support for the Arts

The Filipino arts movement began as a religious movement during the country's earliest days. As churches were built, the faithful wanted to fill them with paintings and sculptures depicting

Komiks are King

Before World War II, comic strips were popular features in most Filipino newspapers. They were a favorite among teens and their parents, with characters and story lines that reflected their lives.

After the war, Filipino "komiks" began to appear as independent publications in colorfully illustrated paperback volumes. By the 1980s, there were more than 50 titles, with some for adults and some for teens.

Today komiks with superheroes and those based on Japanese anime are favorites among Filipino teens. *Darna* is the story of a poor girl with special powers, much like those of Wonder Woman.

While the first komiks provided humor and entertainment, some were published for instruction. The government even used the format to illustrate the latest farming techniques. For Filipino students, komiks are a way to learn history or classic novels. Illustrated, shortened versions of regular books, such as the story of José Rizal, are popular.

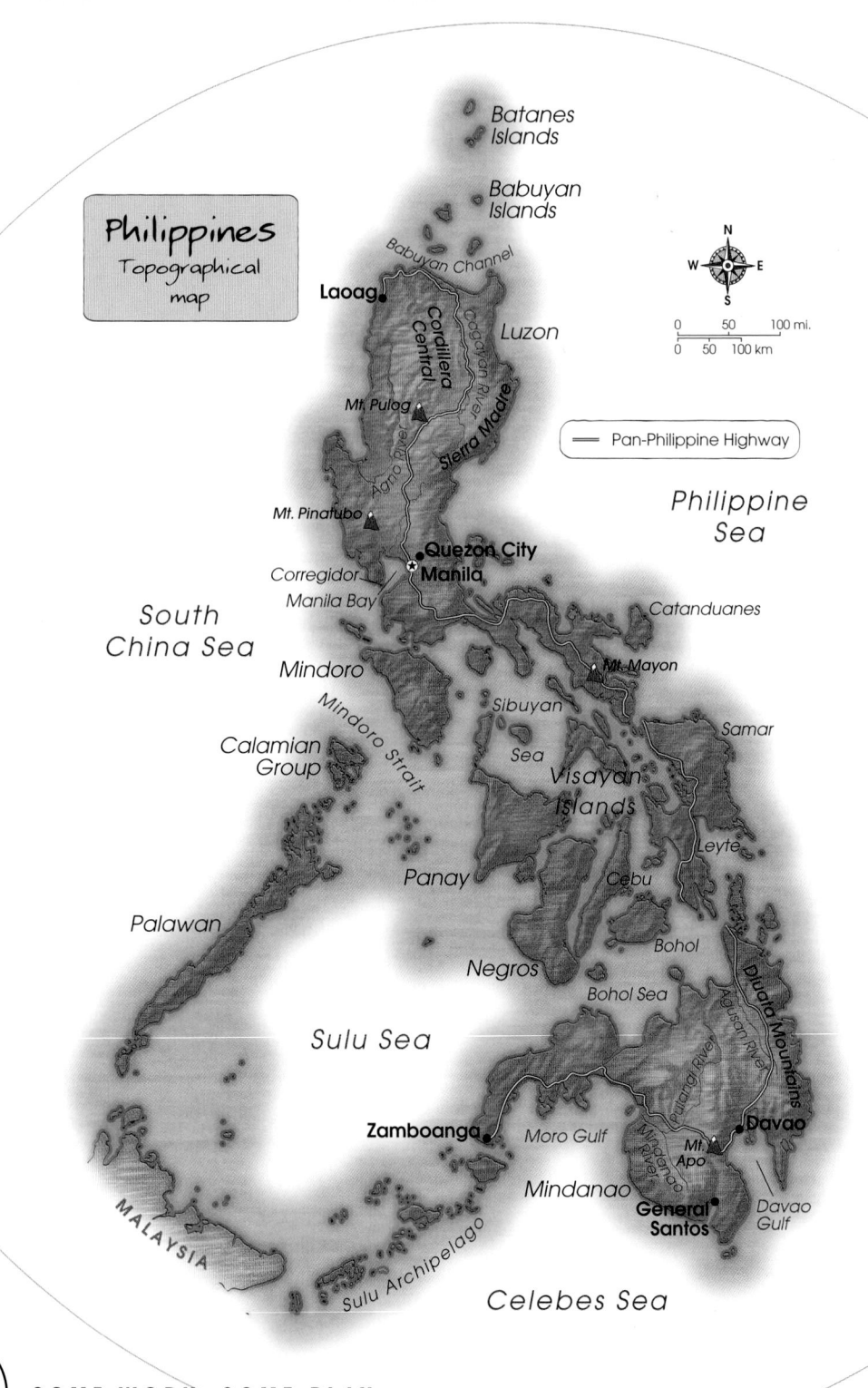

Philippines
Topographical
map

Batanes
Islands

Babuyan
Islands

Babuyan Channel

Laoag

Luzon

Cordillera Central

Cagayan River

Mt. Pulog

Sierra Madre

Agno River

Mt. Pinatubo

Quezon City
Manila

Corregidor

Manila Bay

South
China Sea

Mindoro

Mindoro Strait

Calamian
Group

Palawan

Philippine
Sea

——— Pan-Philippine Highway

Catanduanes

Mt. Mayon

Sibuyan
Sea

Samar

Visayan
Islands

Leyte

Panay

Cebu

Bohol

Negros

Bohol Sea

Diwata Mountains

Agusan River

Sulu Sea

Zamboanga

Moro Gulf

Mindanao River

Pulangi River

Mt. Apo

Davao

Davao
Gulf

MALAYSIA

Sulu Archipelago

Mindanao

General
Santos

Celebes Sea

N
W E
S

0   50   100 mi.
0   50 100 km

The Cultural Center of the Philippines hosts traditional dancers during festivals and celebrations.

stories and people from the Bible. That effort expanded to the creation of secular works that later were displayed in museums.

Today the Filipino government supports art in such places as the National Museum of the Philippines as well as the Cultural Center of the Philippines in Manila. Major Filipino works at the National Museum include Vicente Manansala's *Planting of the Cross*, *Afternoon Scene* by Ricardo Puruganan, and Victorio Edades' *The Sketch*. The

Cultural Center, founded by first lady Imelda Marcos in 1969, trains young musicians and encourages them to seek training and to perform around the world.

The religious movement also helped spawn the Philippines' dramatic arts. Christian plays attracted actors, directors, and playwrights, who later produced nonreligious works.

Young Filipinos go to museums and attend plays for class field trips. They also perform in school and local theater productions.

Looking Ahead

TEENS IN THE PHILIPPINES FACE MANY CHALLENGES. Some have affluent families, live comfortably, and will attend college. Many others live in poverty and have a hard time getting a decent education. Some leave school to work long hours for little pay. Whatever their circumstances, though, most teens take their life in stride and with a smile. They are supported by large, loving families and surrounded by a wide circle of friends. They honor their country's rich history while embracing modern technology and Western ways. They respect each other's sense of pride and are always ready for a good time. For many, their upbeat outlook on life helps them succeed in spite of the hurdles they face. Teens throughout the Philippines are eager and happy to move their country forward through education and hard work.

Official name: Republic of the Philippines

Capital: Manila

People

Population: 91,077,287

Population by age group:
0–14 years: 34.5%
15–64 years: 61.3%
65 years and older: 4.1%

Life expectancy at birth: 70.51 years

Official language: Filipino (based on Tagalog) and English

Other common languages: Cebuano, Ilocano, Hiligaynon (Ilonggo), Bicol, Waray, Pampango, and Pangasinan

Religion:

Roman Catholic: 80.9%	Aglipayan: 2%
Muslim: 5%	Other: 1.8%
Other Christian: 4.5%	Unspecified: 0.6%
Evangelical: 2.8%	None: 0.1%
Iglesia ni Kristo: 2.3%	

Legal ages
Alcohol consumption: 18
Driver's license: 17
Employment: 18 for full employment;
15 if nonhazardous conditions
Leave school: 12
Marriage: 18 with consent of parents; otherwise 21
Military service: 18
Voting: 18

Government

Type of government: Republic

Chief of state: President

Head of government: President elected by popular vote for a six-year term

Lawmaking body: Bicameral Congress composed of Senate and House of Representatives

Administrative divisions: 81 provinces and 136 chartered cities

Independence: June 12, 1898 (from Spain); July 4, 1946 (from United States)

National symbols:
National flower: Sampaguita
National animal: Carabao
National bird: Philippine eagle

Geography

Total Area: 120,000 square miles (300,000 square kilometers)

Climate: Tropical marine; northeast monsoon (November to April); southwest monsoon (May to October)

Highest point: Mount Apo, 9,748 feet (2,954 meters)

Lowest point: Philippine Sea, sea level

Major rivers and lakes: Pasig River, Cagayan River, Laguna de Bay Lake

Major landforms: 7,107 islands; geography is mostly mountains with narrow to broad coastal lowlands

Economy

Currency: Philippine peso

Population below poverty line: 40%

Major natural resources: timber, petroleum, nickel, cobalt, silver, gold, salt, copper

Major agricultural products: sugarcane, coconuts, rice, corn, bananas, cassavas, pineapples, mangoes, pork, eggs, beef, fish

Major exports: semiconductors and electronic products, transportation equipment, garments, copper products, petroleum products, coconut oil, fruits

Major imports: electronic products, mineral fuels, machinery and transport equipment, iron and steel, textile fabrics, grains, chemicals, plastic

Historical Timeline

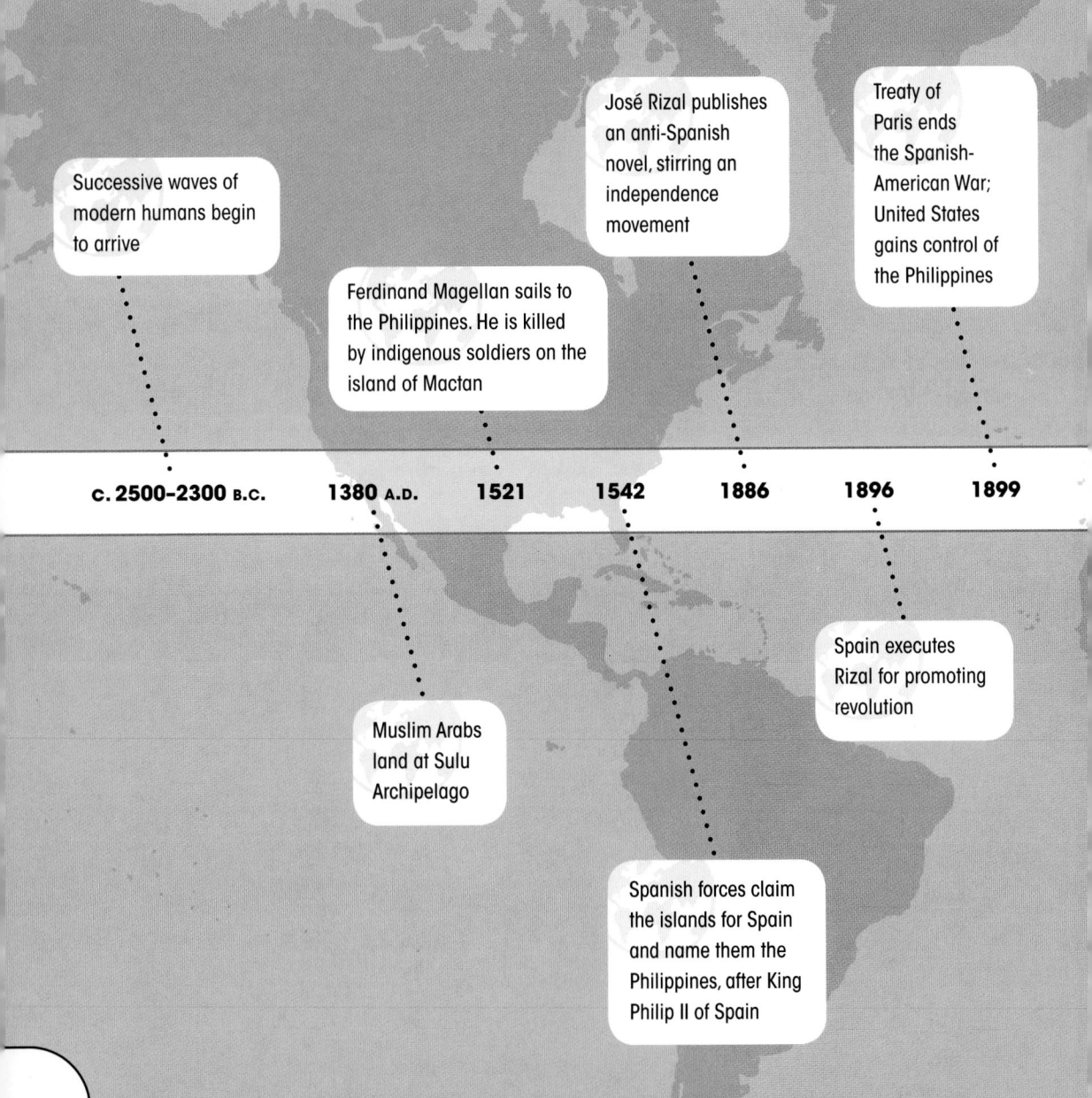

Successive waves of modern humans begin to arrive

Ferdinand Magellan sails to the Philippines. He is killed by indigenous soldiers on the island of Mactan

José Rizal publishes an anti-Spanish novel, stirring an independence movement

Treaty of Paris ends the Spanish-American War; United States gains control of the Philippines

c. 2500–2300 B.C.   **1380 A.D.**   **1521**   **1542**   **1886**   **1896**   **1899**

Muslim Arabs land at Sulu Archipelago

Spain executes Rizal for promoting revolution

Spanish forces claim the islands for Spain and name them the Philippines, after King Philip II of Spain

U.S. Congress promises Philippine independence by 1946; transition to independence begins

The United States gives the Philippines independence; Manuel Roxas is elected the first president of the new republic

Japanese invade the Philippines, defeating American General Douglas MacArthur

| 1902 | 1934 | 1935 | 1941 | 1945 | 1946 | 1972 |

Filipinos are allowed to study in America, helping modernize and westernize the country

Martial law is declared by President Ferdinand E. Marcos

Filipino people approve a constitution creating the Philippine Commonwealth

MacArthur liberates Manila; President Osmeña restores the commonwealth government

Historical Timeline

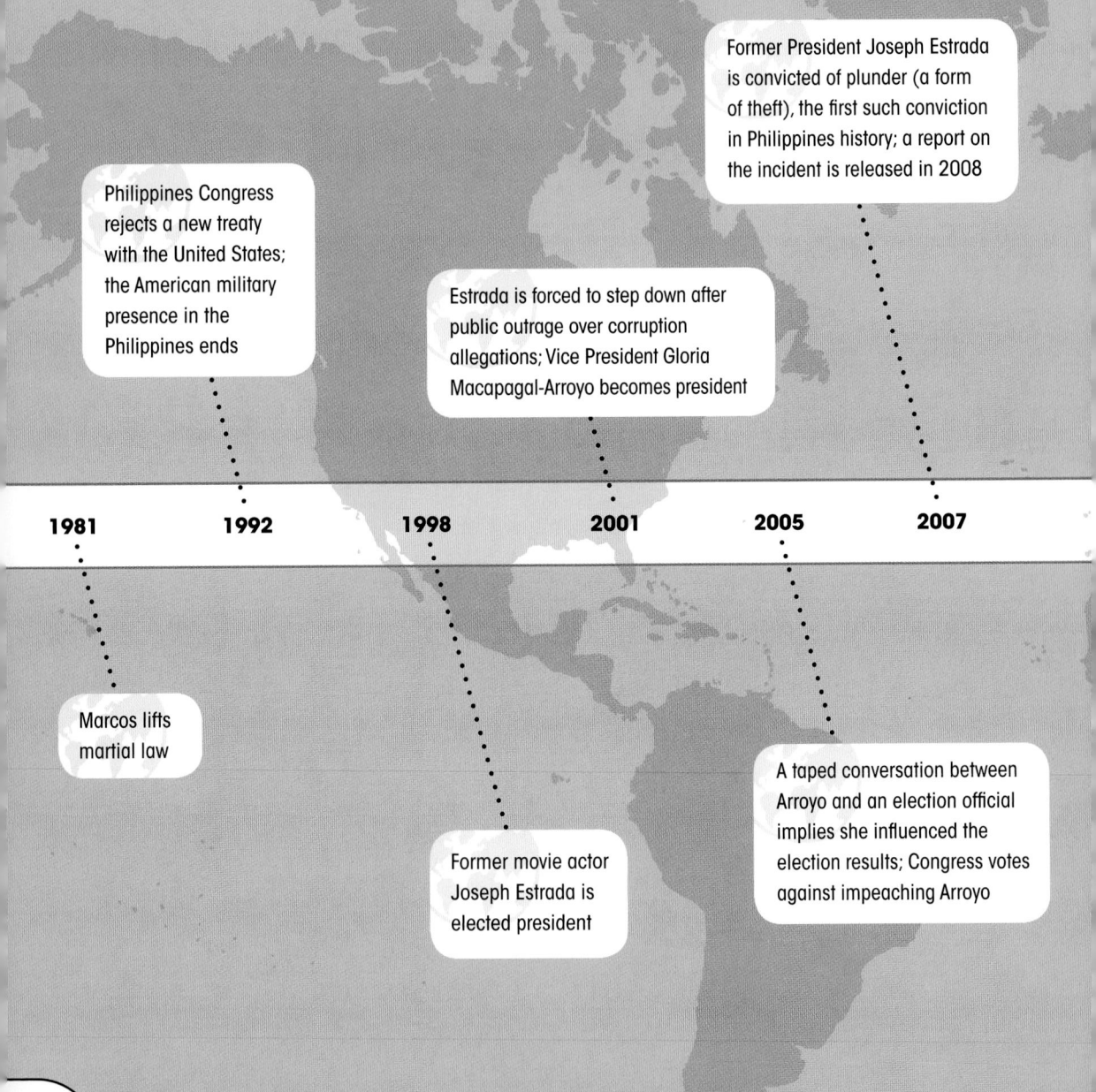

Former President Joseph Estrada is convicted of plunder (a form of theft), the first such conviction in Philippines history; a report on the incident is released in 2008

Philippines Congress rejects a new treaty with the United States; the American military presence in the Philippines ends

Estrada is forced to step down after public outrage over corruption allegations; Vice President Gloria Macapagal-Arroyo becomes president

1981   **1992**   **1998**   **2001**   **2005**   **2007**

Marcos lifts martial law

A taped conversation between Arroyo and an election official implies she influenced the election results; Congress votes against impeaching Arroyo

Former movie actor Joseph Estrada is elected president

Glossary

dialect | form of a language that is spoken in a particular area or by a particular group of people

durian | species of fruit native to southeast Asia; known for its pungent odor

hunter-gatherers | people who hunt, fish, and gather food to survive

infant mortality | number of infant deaths per 100 live births

monsoon | weather seasons characterized by very heavy rainfall

rattan | sturdy vinelike plant used to make furniture

rice terrace | steps built into mountains to grow rice and irrigate crops

secular | not religious; trusting science and knowledge over faith in God

Tagalog | native language of the Philippines

tsunami | gigantic ocean wave created by an undersea earthquake, landslide, or volcanic eruption

typhoon | tropical cyclone; also known as a hurricane

Additional Resources

IN THE LIBRARY

Fiction and nonfiction titles to further enhance your introduction to teens in the Philippines, past and present.

Romulo, Liana Elena, and de Leon, Joanne. *Filipino Children's Favorite Stories*. North Clarendon, Utah: Tuttle Publishing: Periplus Editions, 2000.

Santacroce, John P. *Nine Thousand Miles to Adventure: The Story of an American Boy in the Philippines*. San Antonio: Four Oaks Pub., 1998.

Frank, Sarah. *Filipinos in America*. Minneapolis: Lerner Publications Co., 2006.

Gray, Shirley Wimbish. *The Philippines*. New York: Children's Press, 2003.

Nickles, Greg. *Philippines: The People*. New York: Crabtree Publishing Co., 2002.

Slater, Judith J. *Teen Life in Asia*. Westport, Conn.: Greenwood Press, 2004.

ON THE WEB

For more information on this topic, use FactHound.

1. Go to *www.facthound.com*
2. Type in this book ID: 075653853X
3. Click on the Fetch It button.

Look for more Global Connections books.

Teens in Australia	*Teens in France*	*Teens in Morocco*	*Teens in Spain*
Teens in Brazil	*Teens in Ghana*	*Teens in Nepal*	*Teens in the U.S.A.*
Teens in Canada	*Teens in India*	*Teens in Nigeria*	*Teens in Turkey*
Teens in China	*Teens in Iran*	*Teens in Peru*	*Teens in Venezuela*
Teens in Cuba	*Teens in Israel*	*Teens in Russia*	*Teens in Vietnam*
Teens in Egypt	*Teens in Japan*	*Teens in Saudi Arabia*	
Teens in England	*Teens in Kenya*	*Teens in South Africa*	
Teens in Finland	*Teens in Mexico*	*Teens in South Korea*	

Source Notes

Page 19, photo caption, line 4: Natalie Minev. "Valley student finds similarities between American, Filipino teens during trip to Philippines. *The Review Journal.* 6 April 2004. 20 Feb. 2008. www.reviewjournal.com/lvrj_home/2004/Apr-06-Tue-2004/living/23424804.html

Page 23, column 1, line 13: "How Do Filipino Teenagers While Their Time Away?" *Yahoo! Canadian Answers.* August 2007. 15 Feb. 2008. http://ca.answers.yahoo.com/answers2/frontend.php/question?qid=20070810014209AAU04uL&show=7

Page 25, column 2, line 18: "Durian." *Philippine Herbal Medicine.* 1 Jan. 2008. 20 Feb. 2008. www.philippineherbalmedicine.org/durian.htm

Page 52, sidebar, column 1, line 17: Robyn Eckhardt. "The Dish: Lechon. Manila's Meaty Favorite Spells P-A-R-T-Y." *The Wall Street Journal.* 28 Sept. 2007. 20 Feb. 2008. http://online.wsj.com/article/SB119075618625939123.html?mod=googlenews_wsj

Page 69, column 1, line 4: Joanne L. Rondilla and Paul Spickard. "She Wants to Be Lighter." *Is Lighter Better? Skin-Tone Discrimination Among Asian-Americans.* Lanham, Md.: Rowman & Littlefield Publishers, Inc., p. 55. 1 March 2008. http://books.google.com/books?id=t-JLtPfRjnEC&printsec=copyright&dq=skin+color+philippines+racism+roots+lighter&source=gbs_toc_s&cad=1#PPA55,M1

Page 75, column 1, line 20: "How Do Filipino Teenagers While Their Time Away?"

Pages 84–85, At A Glance: United States Central Intelligence Agency. *The World Factbook—The Philippines.* 12 Feb. 2008. 20 Feb. 2008. www.cia.gov/library/publications/the-world-factbook/geos/rp.html

Select Bibliography

"Child Labour and IPEC: An Overview." *International Labour Organization: International Programme on the Elimination of Child Labour*. 26 Sept. 2006. 15 Feb. 2008. www.ilo.org/public/english/region/asro/manila/ipec/about/overview.htm

CIA World Factbook Online. *The Philippines*. 12 Feb. 2008. 19 Feb. 2008. www.cia.gov/library/publications/the-world-factbook/geos/rp.html

Corpuz, Gerry Albert. "Filipinos Face Worsening Job Prospects." *UPI Asia Online*. 1 Feb. 2008. 16 Feb. 2008. www.upiasiaonline. com/Economics/2008/02/01/filipinos_face_worsening_job_prospects/1048/

Doral, Francis, ed. *Philippines*. London: APA, 2000.

Doyle, Mark. "Philippines Suffers Poverty Divide." *BBC News*. 25 Sept. 2005. 25 Jan. 2008. http://news.bbc.co.uk/2/hi/asia-pacific/4245422.stm

Embassy of the Republic of the Philippines. "Filipino Customs." AsianInfo.org. 2000. 18 Feb. 2008. www.asianinfo.org/asianinfo/philippines/pro-family_customs.htm

Ember, Melvin, and Carol R. Ember. *Countries and Their Cultures*. New York: Macmillan Reference USA, 2001.

Marlow-Ferguson, Rebecca, ed. *World Education Encyclopedia: A Survey of Education Systems Worldwide*. Detroit: Gale Group/ Thomson Learning, 2002.

Official Web Site of the Government of the Philippines. "Frontline Services." 31 Jan. 2008. 16 Feb. 2008. www.gov.ph

"Philippine Culture." Pinas: Your Gateway to Philippine Information. 2002. 1 Feb. 2008. http://pinas.dlsu.edu.ph/culture/culture.html

Ramos, Linette C. "Calamity Funds For Flooded School, Other Needs Stalled; Budget Rules Not Followed." *Sun Star Cebu.* 5 Feb. 2008. 20 Feb. 2008. www.sunstar.com.ph/static/ceb/2008/02/05/news/calamity.funds.for.flooded.school.other.needs.stalled.budget.rules.not.followed.html

Roces, Alfredo, and Grace Roces. *Culture Shock! Philippines.* Portland, Ore.: Graphic Arts Center Publishing Co., 1997.

Roth, Marissa. *Burning Heart: A Portrait of the Philippines.* New York: Rizzoli, 1999.

Rowthorn, Chris. *Philippines.* Melbourne, Victoria: Lonely Planet Publications, 2006.

"Rural Poverty in the Philippines." *Ruralpovertyportal.org.* 13 March 2007. 4 Oct. 2007. www.ruralpovertyportal.org/english/regions/asia/phl/index.htm

U.S. Department of State. "The Philippines." 2007. 10 Jan. 2008. www.state.gov/r/pa/ei/bgn/2794.htm

WOW Philippines. "Discover Philippines." *Facts About the Philippines.* 18 Jan. 2008. www.wowphilippines.com.ph/discover/facts.asp

Index

95

About the Author
Jason Skog

Jason Skog lives in Brooklyn, New York, with his wife and son. He has written several books for young readers. He was a newspaper reporter for 11 years and is a freelance author and writer for newspapers and magazines, including *The New York Times*, the *Boston Globe*, the *Baltimore Sun*, and *Gourmet* magazine.

About the Content Adviser
James F. Eder

James F. Eder is professor of anthropology in the School of Human Evolution & Social Change at Arizona State University. He first went to the Philippines as a Peace Corps volunteer assigned to teach high school biology in Puerto Princesa City on Palawan Island. He has returned to Palawan numerous times to conduct anthropological fieldwork, and he has written several books on how development and change have affected the island's rural inhabitants.

border to border · teen to teen · border to border · teen to teen · border to border